SIGRID RIDES

The Story of an Extraordinary Friendship

SIGRID RIDES

An Adventure on Two Wheels

Travis Nelson

RADAR

First published in Great Britain in 2023 by Radar,
an imprint of Octopus Publishing Group Ltd
Carmelite House
50 Victoria Embankment
London EC4Y 0DZ
www.octopusbooks.co.uk

An Hachette UK Company
www.hachette.co.uk

ISBN (Hardback) 978 1 80419 114 9
ISBN (Trade paperback) 978 1 80419 115 6

A CIP catalogue record for this book is available from the British Library.

Printed and bound in UK.

Typeset in 11.5/17.25pt Heldane Text by Jouve (UK), Milton Keynes.

13 5 7 9 10 8 6 4 2

This FSC® label means that materials used
for the product have been responsibly sourced.

To Ylva, who waits at home and is quick with a cuddle despite missing the adventures.

CONTENTS

1

A NEW START

Snow. That magical first flurry that dusts the city. Sigrid hated it. Immediately I could tell from the confused look on her face that she didn't want to step one paw outside the front door.

'Hey Sigi, it's only snow.' I tried to coax her down from the front porch, but she wasn't budging. Instead, she leaned her nose into the chill air and sniffed suspiciously.

'Yeah, I know it's not California, but it's your new home. It snows here,' I pleaded again, but her bright blue eyes gazed up at me as if to say, *Are you out of your tiny mind?*

Already in her two years on the planet, Sigi and I had had many adventures, but I got the feeling this was one experience too far. But with Sigi, I'd learned that patience is a virtue.

'Come on . . .' I tugged lightly on her leash. *Okay, okay!* I could almost hear her say. Eventually, her right paw tentatively padded out, followed by her left. She shook the freezing, wet flakes from each one as she inched her way down the steps, stopping momentarily to regain her confidence.

'That's it, a bit further . . .' I encouraged her, but that day I was already resigned to a short walk around the neighbourhood. Before we'd hit the main road she'd already attempted to turn back several times. At one point she even hunkered down on the pathway like a petulant teenager, immovable from her wintery bed. Her brilliant white coat would have camouflaged her were it not for the miniature red-and-white sweater I'd dressed her in that morning.

Maybe next time, I thought disappointedly as we headed home. After all, over the past few months Sigi had had a whole new world to take in.

It was mid-January 2020 and we were all finding our feet. Myself and my wife Bianca had arrived in London from the US the previous September filled with dreams about the months ahead. A year or so before, I'd got a job working for a company in London's beating business heart. An executive position at an IT start-up, it had been offered to me by an old boss I'd met while working in Silicon Valley. Now, he'd set up in the capital, building a tech platform in financial services.

'I need people I can trust, Travis. Come work for me. I promise we'll have a ton of fun,' Brandon had said when he first pitched me the idea. It was one of those serendipitous approaches – too good to be true. At the time I was between jobs and living off savings. It had been a tough couple of years. Before I knew it, I'd said yes, and prior to this more permanent relocation, I'd worked a year for the company remotely from home in San Francisco. Down the line, the plan had always been to join him.

Now we were here, we wanted to enjoy every moment. Our idea was simple: work; discover London and immerse ourselves in its arts and culture; see the rest of the UK and travel around Europe. *A couple of years' adventure and then maybe we can head home,* we told ourselves. There was never any doubt that our cats Sigrid and Ylva would be joining us. They're family.

The months leading up to our move had been spent packing boxes, renting a storage unit and sifting through which of our belongings were, or were not, being shipped. Fleetingly, there were moments when I'd chewed over what I would miss: lazy afternoon picnics with friends in Golden Gate Park; the sound of waves lapping the dunes on Ocean Beach; the avenues that stretched for miles. Mostly, though, I was fixated on the trip ahead. Finally, a fresh start that could give me the happiness I was searching for.

Much of that preparation time had also been focused on ensuring a safe passage for Sigi and Ylva. Relocating cats is not simple and I'd spent hours researching the best route. Because the UK is an island, its animal entry rules are more stringent than elsewhere in Europe – even more so since Britain left the EU – but the pet health certificate, microchip and vaccination record needed seemed like a minor inconvenience compared to the perils of the journey itself.

We had a choice: either we could fly directly to the UK with the cats travelling in a heated compartment in the cargo hold; or we could ship them separately and retrieve them once they'd cleared customs. I wanted neither. For the last year Sigi and

Ylva had been by my side pretty much every day. And if we ever went on vacation, we'd never put them in a cattery, only allowing trusted people to drop by to feed and play with them.

A search online only reinforced my fears. There were headline horror stories at every click.

CAT OWNER DISTRAUGHT AFTER PET
INJURED IN TRANSIT.
AIRLINE CLOCKS UP HIGHEST PET DEATHS.
CAT ESCAPES AT AIRPORT.

Then, I made the mistake of typing in the question, *What is the best way to relocate your cat from the US to the UK?* on a bunch of pet forums. I waited and then scrolled down. Things didn't normally go wrong on flights, but they *could*. Just like that, animals can disappear. And what's the recourse? Maybe some compensation from an airline if you're lucky. *Can you even sue border control if a pet goes missing in its care?* I typed.

Shipping cats across the Atlantic sounded even more terrifying. Not only would it take longer than a week, but I imagined them locked in a smelly, echoey hold with no one to comfort them if they got distressed. On arrival we could be waiting days, weeks even, for them to be released from the clutches of some Kafkaesque bureaucracy: not quarantine as such, but a laborious processing procedure. We'd miss them too much. Besides, we could never live with our consciences if they came to any harm.

There was only one thing for it. Instead of flying direct to

London, we'd take a detour through Paris, where the rules are looser. That way, we could take them in their carriers on our laps in the cabin. From France we could hop across the English Channel via the Eurotunnel from Calais to Folkestone. For that leg of the trip we could have used a pet courier service but by now any separation was out of the question in my mind. We'd hire a car and take them ourselves.

On the day we left, we dosed them up with gabapentin – a drug handed to us by the vet to calm their anxiety. The journey ahead would be at least 24 hours. There would be passengers and queues, take-offs and touchdowns. As far as I was concerned, the less they experienced of it the better. As soon as they began to zone out and curl up asleep, we placed them in their carriers and said goodbye to the golden state.

I've learned that early fall in London can lull you into a false sense that the summer might never end, and as we arrived in September 2019 the heat had lingered. The trees outside our new apartment were still bursting with leaves and blocked the view of the main road. As we turned the key and stepped in, relief flooded through me.

The flight from San Francisco International had been plain sailing, but the anxiety I'd been stamping down all journey hit once we'd landed in Charles de Gaulle. We picked up our hire car and reached Calais, making constant checks through the wire meshing to see that the cats were still relaxed. They were, but Bianca and I were flustered.

'Have we got all the right documents?' I asked nervously, as we parked up and entered the pet processing building. With its corrugated iron shell, it looked like a miniature IKEA store from the outside and once we'd stepped through its sliding doors, its reception felt clinical, like a vet's surgery.

'I think so, I double-checked, but . . .'

All the meticulous planning we'd done was now plunged into doubt. I became tormented by a nightmare vision of us being delayed and ordered to wait hours in line for further verifications. Or turned away for some other reason we hadn't even considered. As we shuffled through, the officer smiled politely, his eyes quietly inspecting Bianca, then me. Then, he studied Sigrid and Ylva's health certificates – one for the French side and another to get us past customs in the UK. Seconds ticked by.

'Vaccination certificates please,' he stated matter-of-factly in his broken French accent. Carefully, he examined each document. This guard was thorough, and I followed his eyes as they slowly made their way down the page. 'All fine, please walk through,' he smiled and waved us out to pick up our car before boarding. *Seriously? That's it?* I thought. Far less painful than either of us had imagined, but the real test was still to come.

Once we had disembarked in England, I'd have to drive our French left-hand-drive car on the wrong side of the road. And not on wide freeways either, like I was used to in the States. To this day, I've not got used to how narrow and winding the UK's roads are. Or that its cities aren't built on easily navigable grid systems like back home.

Once we hit the Blackwall Tunnel on London's east side, I could feel my stomach clench. What usually came naturally, I now had to think about. My brain did contortions just to work out how to make a right-hand turn at a junction. *What the hell is the correct lane?* Traffic seemed to appear from all directions, drivers pushing their way onwards, angrily beeping their horns. Being mindful of our precious cargo on the back seat – and our fatigue from the journey – only added to the pressure, and my hands gripped the wheel as we entered the labyrinth of roads on the other side. I guess the protector in me wanted us to be safe.

Thankfully, when we reached our new apartment everything felt more friendly – not that it had been so easy to secure. Weeks before our final move, I'd combined a trip to London with a bunch of meetings, and Bianca had flown with me knowing the short window we had to find a place.

We'd scoured online adverts and estate agents' windows. Universally, we were told we were welcome so long as we had the required deposit and proof of income. But our cats? Nah. No pets allowed. *That sucks,* I thought. In San Francisco pet-friendly apartments are far more available, particularly if you're a dog owner. Californians *love* dogs. In the end, our choice got narrowed down to whichever landlord was open to the idea.

One area, Shoreditch in East London, felt like a strong contender. To me, it appeared familiar. As we strolled through its gentrified-but-still-rugged streets and back alleys, I could have been back in the Mission in San Francisco – one of the oldest neighbourhoods in the city, which I'd lived in some years ago. Like Shoreditch, it's now filled with cool restaurants and bars, cocktail lounges and tattoo parlours. Street murals cover the warehouse apartment walls and the vibe is unmistakeably hipster. But the apartment we viewed in Shoreditch didn't have the warmest feel.

Belsize Park, where we ended up, couldn't have looked more different. It felt charming by comparison, leafy and laid-back. To Americans like us, it also felt elegantly English – quaint, we would say – with its period houses and tree-lined streets. Perfect to come home to if we were working, we figured, but also lively enough to hang out in its boutique cafes and bars. The apartment was a little more expensive than we'd planned to pay but still cheaper than the equivalent in San Francisco. Besides, once Bianca found work, we'd be on a decent joint salary.

As days rolled into weeks, I could see Sigi and Ylva loving their new surroundings too. In fact, they took to Belsize Park from the get-go – one less headache for us, and it made us feel even luckier to have found this place. Our apartment in the Sunset District of San Francisco had been on the second floor with the sun streaming in through every window. Outside, there were pedestrians and cars, street lights and traffic signals to gaze at. But here, window-watching reached a whole new level. Sigi and Ylva had been catapulted into the centre of a feline theme park, teeming with urban wildlife.

Likewise, we'd chosen a two-bedroom apartment on the second floor, but this time around the rear of the Victorian terrace overlooked a garden that stretched way back. Oak, sycamore, birch and London plane trees and a whole variety of plants and bushes were home to pigeons, starlings, magpies and blue tits.

'Hey Sig, what are you looking at?' I often asked her. Whenever I gazed up from my laptop I noticed how, from early on, she'd taken up residence on a window ledge, face pressed up to the glass and her eyes darting left then right before her teeth began chattering – cat code for spotting potential prey. I was always intrigued to see which creature she'd developed a fascination for and was following like an engrossing drama on cat TV.

Out front, it was the same. Trees also overhung our North London street and squirrels somersaulted on branches at death-defying heights. Urban foxes were an entirely new phenomenon: stalking around, noses in the trash cans sifting their way through the city's leftovers. We heard them clamber between houses, screeching like babies to attract a mate or scare off predators – an alien sound to us. In San Francisco, only racoons are the garbage scavengers – trash pandas, we call them, because of the black-and-white markings circling their eyes.

Then there was the cat superhighway: the outside ledge of the window in our spare room and the route that other cats from the neighbourhood took to move from house to house and garden to garden. Ginger toms and tabby cats all sauntered along. This was also foreign to us. In fact, it was one of the first things that struck me about the UK: that even in a built-up city like London, owners think nothing of letting their cats roam free. Again, not a common sight stateside. Cats there are mostly house cats. Cat flaps aren't even a thing. Because of that, I'd never witnessed how territorial Sigi could be.

Hey, that's my ledge, I could now hear her hissing as she leaped towards the window furiously swiping out her paw at any cat who dared to pass. Sometimes she'd misjudge the jump or clean forget there was a wall of glass between her and it and bang herself accidentally like a cartoon cat, a halo of imaginary stars spinning above her head. At first the intruders turned, momentarily startled by the white blur hurtling towards them, but after a while they didn't care. Nonchalantly, the cats wandered on.

Admittedly, in those first two months after arriving, I didn't take Sigi or Ylva outside much at all. Being present at work was full-on. Having spent a year staring at a computer screen from my study at home, I'd almost forgotten what it was like to travel to an office. It had its upsides, I decided.

My official title was Director of Cloud and Mobile Data. I'd spent most of my adult life in the abstract world of computer programming and data management and this role was no different, although like any start-up my day-to-day reality was much more fluid. The company managed clients' payrolls through a tech platform and while my department had initially consisted of me, we'd now grown to a team of five. A bunch of staff worked from the office in London, but others checked in remotely from around the world. We had software engineers as far away as Brazil and Canada.

As workplaces go, it was pretty relaxed – not the hard-driving environment I'd experienced so often in Silicon Valley. Invites to drinks after work happened almost immediately, helped along by the office being part of a large co-working space with a kitchen complete with self-serve bar on each floor – a ready-made social life to slot into. And many of my contemporaries weren't natives of the UK at all. In my team, Ryan had been in London for a while but had grown up in the Pacific Northwest around the Seattle area, similar to me. We clicked straight away given we were both news junkies. Over the past years he'd watched from across the pond the rise of Donald Trump and the Republican far right, and many of our conversations revolved around how polarized debate had become in our country. And how, since Britain left Europe, the same seemed to be spreading here.

And Oskar had arrived from Norway. He was a gentle giant who spent most of his spare time weightlifting. I would describe him as 'aggressively nice' – the type of guy who asked 'How was your weekend?' and genuinely cared about the answer. For me, the international melting pot could make work extra complicated, but far more interesting as we navigated each other's cultural differences and language quirks.

Every morning I boarded the 168 bus that went directly to the centre of London from Haverstock Hill, a two-minute walk from our apartment. As it wound its way through the market streets of Camden and on past the Georgian terraces of Bloomsbury, I stared out. I was mesmerized by how London had evolved and remained in constant flux. Social housing sat side by side with well-to-do residential blocks and offices. In other areas, cranes filled the skyline like beacons of regeneration and renewal. At rush hour, people flowed like electrical currents through a network of interconnected nerve centres, all with their own lives and stories and experiences of this vast metropolis. At times, the sheer size of London overwhelmed me.

And while I looked forward to the daily commute, what was frustrating was how it now stole chunks of my day that would normally be spent taking Sigi out for a walk. It was something I'd always done. But if a man with a cat on a leash is not a regular sight in the UK, it's also not a common occurrence in San Francisco. Yet I thought that Sigi shouldn't be confined to house cat status. Nor Ylva, although she never took to walks in the same way. I wanted their lives to be enriched by the smells and sounds and sights that indoor cats were deprived of: to have the best start in life that I could provide for them. After all, I was their guardian.

I still remember those first walks out with Sigi. She must have been only a few months old when I introduced her to the great outdoors. In preparation, I'd ordered a harness for her – a funky leopard-skin design. If Sigi was stepping out with me, she was never going to look boring. I always wanted to have fun with Sigi and so I dressed her in a fun way too.

The run-up to our first outing took several weeks. When the harness arrived, with a leash attached, it was so oversized it swamped her tiny body, and I could tell she wasn't too pleased about wearing it, either. 'Here Sig, look what I've got for you,' I said, allowing her to sniff it and rub her cheek against the velvet material to ease her in gently.

The main body of the harness fastened under Sigi's tummy by way of a Velcro strap and another strap sat loosely around her neck. I figured the sensation of wearing it might feel uncomfortable so I took it stage by stage. At first, I laid the material over the arch of her back for a few minutes every day. *What the hell is this?* Her face said it all, and she immediately bristled and tried to shake it off.

'It's okay Sig. It won't hurt.' I petted her head reassuringly. She looked up unconvinced and I watched as her tail dropped low between her legs – a sure sign she was feeling anxious.

The next day, I tried again. 'Hey Sigi, one more time,' I told her. But as soon as I fell to my knees and pulled out the harness, she scowled and backed away. Then, she sat motionless just staring at it. I wondered whether she thought it was prey or if she could make out much detail about it at all. Yet, I also sensed her curiosity. Sure enough, after a few more tries she slowly crept towards it. This time, when I laid it over her back she let it rest.

'Good girl Sigi.' I rewarded her with tickles under her chin and soft scratches around her ears. Over the next few days, I managed to get the under-tummy strap fastened without her attempting to wriggle out of it. Then, I progressed to around her neck, but she shook her head violently and tried to lift the collar off with her paw. Yet gradually, she allowed me to go further. When she sat blinking contentedly with the harness fully secured, I knew she was ready. And using the same patient method, I encouraged Sigi outside.

At first, she sat transfixed by the open front door, basking in the wall of heat that hit us whenever it was open. Then, one day she took a few steps. The next day, she took some more, until finally we made it down the alleyway and out through the end gate. Suddenly, the view she'd only ever seen from the window came alive in full technicolour. As she took a front-row seat on the kerbside, her head swayed from side to side as she followed the traffic cruising up and down.

It took around a month before Sigi could manage a full circuit around the block. But what I hadn't factored in was that Sigi turned out to be the slowest walker on the planet. If I'd kept to her pace, I'd never have got back in time for work. She had a quiet inquisitiveness about everything on the route. Sometimes she would sit and stare at grasses and plants. She took great pleasure in rubbing herself against palms. Cactuses surprised her, and she jerked her head back if her nose got too close and hit a prickle. Somehow, though, it never stopped her going back.

'Hey, time to go.' I always gave the leash two quick tugs, but I could see her eyes roll. *You brought me all this way and now it's time to go?* 'Yup, time to go Sig. Sorry . . .' A last resort was to lift her up and carry her.

It wasn't long before Sigi got used to our daily strolls. I tried to time them for when she was awake and fully alert, and I noticed that after she'd come round from a long sleep she began asking me to go out. She'd circle around my legs and rub her tail against them. Or she'd wait by the office door and miaow, turning back to check if I'd made a move from my chair. On other occasions, I would find her by the front door gazing up expectantly.

We took in longer distances. Once round the block became two blocks. If we wanted to go further, I put her in a chest harness, like you would a newborn baby. It fastened around my torso and I slotted her in with her back resting against my chest and her paws dangling out. Again, she seemed unsure of it at first but she quickly loved the warmth of my body against hers, which seemed to calm her.

Having the chest harness meant I could expand her horizons further. Golden Gate Park, three blocks down, became our regular go-to. There, I'd take her out of the chest harness and attach her leash so she could roam freely and sniff around. For the next half hour she stared at plants and craned her head upwards at the trees. Monterey cypresses with their squat trunks and low branches became her favourite, and the first time she got close to one I felt her tug hard on the leash, as if instinct was pulling her.

'You want to climb, Sigi?' I brought her closer to its trunk and loosened off the leash a little. Within seconds she was up on her hind legs, her claws digging into the bark and her tail flicking from side to side with sheer pleasure. If warblers or hummingbirds flew overhead, she became almost dizzy with excitement, as if she was overloaded with stimuli.

As we settled into our new life in London, I had it in my mind to give Sigi exactly the same kinds of experiences I had done back then – only I knew doing so would eat into time I didn't always have. Our number of clients was growing week by week and being present every day began to feel far more re-energizing than working remotely had ever done. The office fizzed with the enthusiasm of a young start-up. There would be time for Sigi and I to discover our new surroundings I told myself. For now, I needed to thrive.

2

PAST HISTORIES

By the end of January, the snow had long gone. Now it was drizzling, and dark, but our lives in London had got brighter. It hadn't taken long for Bianca to find work in a mobile gaming company in Shoreditch, and she'd been there for around three months. Plus, we'd made some friends locally.

That winter, we'd been forced to explore beyond our flat through necessity more than anything else. Our belongings took months to ship and we didn't want to buy duplicates of kitchen equipment or furniture that would be turning up any time soon. We had our limits, though. We could almost put up with being hunched on the living room floor with our laptops perched on our knees, but after a few nights of sleeping on the hard wooden boards in our bedroom, we caved in and invested in a new mattress. Without a duvet we'd got into the habit of crashing out under a large blanket topped with the thick, plastic mattress cover to keep the warmth in.

Cooking dinner also felt like a mission, so it was no accident that we started to become regulars at the pub at the top of our street – The Washington. The traditional English pub is something I'd experienced before on trips to London, but then I'd felt like a tourist. At home too, there's a handful of English-themed bars serving pints of Fuller's ale and steak and kidney pies. But on America's West Coast, where the temperature rarely drops below 8°C all winter, the atmosphere is hardly authentic. Now, with its cosy snugs and wood-burning fires, The Washington became like a second home, a refuge where we could reflect on the day and continue to acclimatize.

One evening, not long after we'd arrived, a stocky-looking guy with a warm-hearted smile bounded over to us. 'Hey, I see you guys have moved in downstairs,' he grinned.

'Sure,' I replied, curious as to who he was. I hadn't seen him in the hallway.

'I'm Alexis', he continued, 'but call me Lexi', he said, holding out his hand. Before we knew it, he'd pulled up a chair and was filling us in on the neighbourhood. He looked in his late twenties and he lived upstairs with his mum, Mary. 'Know who we have as neighbours?' he leaned in. His eyes were sparkling. Bianca and I had no clue. We'd chosen our apartment without ever thinking of who we'd be living next to. At home, we didn't even know our neighbours. People tended to keep to their own families or friendship cliques.

'Who?' I stared at him inquisitively.

'I shouldn't say,' he smiled teasingly, but he lasted all of two seconds before he couldn't stop himself from blabbing.

'Helena Bonham Carter. The actress. You know her?'

Sure, I knew her. I only had to think of any British movie I'd ever seen, like the *Harry Potter* series, the period drama *A Room with a View* and a whole slew of other blockbusters like *Planet of the Apes*.

'You're kidding, right?'

'Nope,' he smiled again. Our area and nearby Primrose Hill was awash with celebrities, he explained. It was *the* place to hang out. On any day of the week, you might see Noel Gallagher from the Britpop band Oasis bowling down England's Lane. Or the model Kate Moss, or any number of A-listers going about their business.

'And now it has me and Bianca. The paparazzi will be beating down our door,' I said with a heavy dose of sarcasm, which made Lexi laugh.

'Good choice of pub.' He nodded approvingly, before heading back to the bar. Apparently, we could find him there several nights of the week. And, after that, we'd run into him often.

At the other end of the street was the Sir Richard Steele – a historic pub with an equally homely feel which we called simply 'the Steele'. It had been the long-time home of its namesake, a local celebrity himself and the founder of the English high-society gossip magazine *Tatler*. It still had an English grandeur about it but it felt anything but stuffy inside. It's bald and burley Irish manager, Stephen, welcomed us enthusiastically and made a point of coming over to chat every time we were in. Jazmin, one of the bartenders, was also a super-friendly face. A petite but coarse-humoured Canadian with a liking for Scotch, she'd often sit with us after last orders and nurse a glass as she unwound after her shift.

Before I lived here, so many people told me that London can be a hostile city – too many folk racing around with no time for anyone, but so far I'd not experienced it that way at all, and these early interactions only confirmed my view.

But as we were developing a social life, I was acutely aware that Sigi and Ylva were adjusting to more solitary days. Whereas previously one of us would have been at home, we now left for work by 10am and often didn't arrive back until some time after 7pm. From the stairwell, I could hear both cats miaowing at operatic levels before I'd even put the key in the lock. *A bit melodramatic,* I thought, but I also understood. They'd got used to being stroked and pampered on a daily basis, and now the flat was bare and empty. I couldn't help feel a pang of guilt every time I looked down at their disappointed faces.

'Hey, how's your day been?' I greeted both with a head pat and a friendly rub to the back of their necks, but it was Sigi who would follow me around like a lost soul for the rest of the evening. She'd jump up on to my shoulders, or nuzzle her face against my legs, clearly wanting to make up for lost time. 'I'm sorry Sig. I'll take you out for a walk soon,' I promised.

While Bianca and I share both cats, Ylva definitely claimed Bianca as her own from early on. Sigi, on the other hand, was unquestionably mine and it's only recently that she's been able to sit on Bianca's lap and snuggle for any time at all. It had always been that way, ever since the first day we brought her home in the summer of 2017.

That summer I'd slept on a makeshift bed beside Sigi in our spare
room for close to a month. She couldn't have been bigger than a
kilogram bag of sugar and her hair felt as soft as a ball of cotton
wool. I wanted to make sure that she felt settled and secure in
her new environment. *Imagine being this small and alone at
night in a strange place?* I thought. Also, I had a suspicion that
Ylva – our first feline occupant, a Bengal breed and a far more
nervy cat – might bully her and try to show her who was boss.
After all, our San Francisco apartment had been her sole domain
for more than three years.

Over those first few days, Sigi and I bonded. As well as
sleeping beside her, I was also doing my day job dialling into
work every morning. The minute she saw my fingers tapping
on the keyboard, she hopped up on to the desk and sniffed
around before curling up to sleep, usually resting beside or on
the keyboard itself. Or she nestled into my feet under the desk.
Whenever she was feeling playful, she hopped up on top of the
monitor and peeked over the screen to catch my attention. It
didn't take much. I was besotted with Sigi from day one.

Also apparent was her sense of adventure, even before I
started taking Sigi out for walks. We'd caught a first glimpse of
that spirit on the ride home from the breeder after we picked her
up. She was so tiny that we'd let her roam free around the car for
the duration of the journey.

'Hey Sigi, you can sit here,' I'd encouraged her, tapping my
thigh. At first, she seemed hesitant and stared up, carefully
reading my eyes. But a few short steps later and she laid in the
crease between my legs while I drove. At intervals she woke,

stretched out her back legs and balanced her front paws on the base of the steering wheel. The steady vibration of the engine seemed to transport her to a world of her own. And when she eventually got bored, Bianca and I watched in amazement as she scaled the dashboard and created a makeshift lookout between it and the windscreen – a perfect vantage point to follow cars on the road ahead.

I wonder whether Sigi's life now was always meant to be – whether she is hardwired for adventure, or whether our friendship created it. Nature or nurture? I guess I'll never know. Certainly, it took several adventures for us to find each other. Sigrid is a Norwegian Forest cat who had been present in my imagination ever since I'd travelled to Scandinavia in the summer of 2016, the year before she came into my life.

Back then, I'd gone on a spur-of-the moment trip to trace my family tree. While many White Americans like to proudly consider themselves as pure-blood natives, none are. In truth, though, I'd always felt the opposite. Having grown up in rural America, any inkling that the Nelsons were more interesting than the hillbilly world they revolved around fascinated me. And while I didn't know much, I knew that my grandparents on my father's side had emigrated from Norway. Like so many others, they'd followed in the footsteps of the early 19th-century pioneers who'd arrived in North Dakota. Then, Norwegian settlers flocked to the plains of the Sheyenne River Valley and the Red River Valley that stretched all the way up to the Canadian border. Apparently, the brush landscape and rocky mountains reminded them of home and they set up farms across the vast prairies. Over time families like mine had spread out, some gravitating to the Pacific Northwest to the urban centres of Seattle and the wilderness of Washington State, where I was born and mainly raised.

All I remember of my grandparents is that they were strong, silent types: a manner that could be confused with stand-offishness, but I decided masked a stoicism born from enduring short days and long, brutal winters in Norway. They vowed they would never go back. Maybe it's what also gave them an air of mystery and drove me to want to learn more about that branch of the family: a hidden past that nobody else in my family seemed to care too much about at all.

That summer I used my vacation for a trip around Europe and combined it with connecting with friends. Many years before I'd studied in Belgium and I'd kept in touch with a few people. By then I'd already traced our Norse name, Nilsen, back to a farm deep within a region in eastern Norway called Valdres. I hadn't yet been able to pinpoint the farm's exact location, I didn't even know if it still existed, but given that I'd planned to visit Norway regardless, I decided to go out of curiosity. After a couple of nights in Oslo, I headed north and after a long morning on the road, I pulled up in the remote village of Bagn and took my chances in a local store to see if anyone could help.

Walking inside felt like opening the door on an armoury. Industrial chainsaws hung from the ceilings and a patchwork of axes and saws covered the walls. I gulped at the array of potential weaponry. A middle-aged guy stood behind the counter dressed in military fatigues.

'Hey man, I'm looking for a farm where my family might have lived.' For all I knew the Nelsons, our adapted name once we'd arrived in the US, could still have relatives living there. It seemed a long shot, but for the whole journey I'd felt consumed by the fantasy.

He looked me up and down. 'What's the name?'

'Nilsen.'

'Nilsen.' He paused and chewed the side of his lip. 'Used to hunt with a guy by that name. Years back. Family were farming here,' he said, pointing vaguely west.

'Seriously?' I could feel a buzz of excitement rush through me.

They hunted wild lynx together, he continued, and after the hunts they held parties on the clifftops nearby. It didn't take long before his initial reserve had vanished and he was offering to take me there.

'Sure. I'd love that,' I said.

'Don't know who owns it now.' He shrugged.

The short drive to the spot was lined with evergreen trees. As soon as the main road petered out, we veered on to a track road. We'd have to travel the rest by foot, my new guide Kjetil told me, instructing me to pull up before the pathway disappeared completely. Five minutes later and we'd reached a clearing where a wooden shack stood on the far side of a grass meadow. Even from a distance, it was clear it wasn't inhabited and as I walked closer an unease crept through me. Its exterior wooden panels were dry and weathered and the red paint on the corrugated iron roof had mostly peeled. The windows were smashed.

When I peered inside my fears turned to an overwhelming sadness. It seemed like whoever had lived there had suddenly upped and left. Bedsheets and clothes still hung from an indoor washing line strung up in the kitchen; a pottery vase sat on a central dining table. Black-and-white photographs hung lopsided on the faded blue walls. Part of me wanted to step inside and rummage through its dusty cupboards and display cabinets, but I stopped myself. This felt like someone's home – maybe my family home. It felt disrespectful to intrude, even though it was clearly derelict.

I came away from Valdres desperate to know more, but unsure of what else I could find. Not ready to give up, I left my details with my new friend, thanked him for his time and headed back to Oslo, and eventually home to the US. But the eeriness of the farm remained in my mind for weeks. Then one day, I logged on to my email to find a message. Kjetil had been sleuthing. He'd talked to someone locally who had known the farm's last occupants. It wasn't much to go on, but I was grateful.

A couple of months later he got in contact again. This time, he'd searched through land records and stumbled on a lead to a potential owner – a professor of linguistics at Oslo University. And when I wrote to her, she confirmed that she'd inherited the farm from my great-grandfather, but without someone willing to farm the land, it had fallen into ruin.

It would be another two years before she and I would meet face to face, but having that deep-rooted connection to my

Norwegian past somehow made me feel special. I'd never been close to my parents growing up and, as an only child, I'd felt like a bit of a misfit. To me, family seemed like a remote entity. But this family seemed colourful and fascinating.

In my mind, Sigi also became another link to that past. Subconsciously, I think I sought her out. As soon as I planned on taking on another cat, her Norwegian long-haired breed jumped out at me online. Forest cats have unruly manes that look almost like a lion's and I was drawn to the pictures immediately. When I scrolled down the page of the Cat Fanciers' Association website – the cat bible in the US – I learned about her pedigree and made up my mind there and then. Apparently, Norwegian Forest cats date all the way back to the Viking Age to around A D 800. They even feature in an ancient Norse fairy tale, when two cats pulled the chariot of the goddess Freya. The breed had almost been lost in the past, due to cross-breeding, but had been brought back from the brink of extinction. But Forest cats didn't arrive on US shores until 1979.

Maybe that's why tracking down Sigi proved almost impossible. Bengals like Ylva are easy to find in Southern California, as are American Shorthair cats and even breeds like Siamese. But Norwegian Forest cats aren't top of any breeders' lists, and it took me weeks to eventually stumble on one. Melissa, a breeder who lived in Hermosa Beach on the south side of Los Angeles bred only Norwegian Forest cats and when I dropped her a line she told me that her new litter had not long been born.

Most had already been reserved by would-be owners, but one cat hadn't. She sent over a picture.

Wow. What struck me immediately was the brilliant white colouring of Sigi's coat – a kitten so beautiful and unusual that I couldn't stop staring at her. Melissa explained that this kitten was the last of the litter, but that her father Shalu was a prize-winning pedigree who had won several awards at cat shows across the state. If I wanted her, she was mine, but we wouldn't be able to bring her home until she was at least three months old and ready to be adopted. I remembered an Old Norse name I'd read somewhere and liked – Sigrid – meaning 'beautiful victory'. It would suit her perfectly I decided, and I named her Sigrid before we'd even met.

In the months before I could bring Sigi home, Melissa continued to send pictures and cute little videos. Each one made me want to meet Sigi even more, and it also gave me a good feeling about Melissa. In truth, when you buy from breeders it can be hit and miss. Certainly, the breeder I bought Ylva from was not reputable at all but until I'd made the trip there it had been very hard to tell. Loveable pictures online can hide a multitude of sins but given how cheap Ylva was I probably should have guessed. Now, I don't believe Ylva had the best of starts in life at all. She was also the runt of the litter, but when I arrived to pick her up I found her shut in a cage cowering alone and frightened in a dark shed. Other cats were charging recklessly around the breeder's house, and the stench of stale cat pee attacked my nostrils the minute I walked in, as if the carpets had never been washed. I never could get my head around why people so cruel become breeders. Surely there's a better way to earn money than to keep animals in such awful conditions?

Ylva was also very hesitant to be petted, only creeping forward after I'd kneeled down for several minutes with my hand outstretched, and it made me suspect that maybe she'd never been out of that cage since birth. All I wanted to do was scoop her up and take her to where she would be loved and cared for. I named her after reading a bestselling novel called *The Long Ships* – an epic written by Scandinavian storyteller Frans G Bengtsson, set during the Viking raids on the UK in the late 10th century. Just like Sigrid, the name kind of stuck; it means she-wolf. Without doubt, Ylva was, and is, high maintenance and jokingly my then-girlfriend and I also christened her the 'budget Bengal'.

The day Bianca and I picked up Sigi I couldn't help feeling anxious. This time, my fingers were firmly crossed that she'd been well cared for as any new kitten deserves. We set off early, arriving in Hermosa Beach in the afternoon after a seven-hour drive. A few blocks back from the golden coastline, Melissa's house looked ordinary enough. And when she answered, any concerns I had fell away.

'Hi, lovely to see you. I've been waiting.' She beamed and invited us in. There was no smell of cat pee, no animals running around and no cages. *Thank God,* I thought. Furthermore, Melissa turned out to be super-sweet, just like her messages in the few months leading up to meeting her. As we talked she reminded me of a typical wine mom: a glamorous stay-at-home wife with perfect make-up and polished nails who bred cats and enjoyed a glass or four every evening. When I looked around her place it wasn't pristine, but it was clean and warm and homely.

'Here she is.' Melissa led us through to the living room. Sigi was smaller than I had imagined and as I bent down to say hi she immediately glanced up and ambled over to be stroked.

'Hey there.' I gently patted her head. She was way more beautiful than in her photos and videos. I could also tell that she'd been well looked after. Keeping watch from the sofa was her father Shalu who was a large and muscular tom but whose coat was immaculate, and it reassured me that Melissa was a very attentive breeder.

'I handle all the kittens right from birth,' she told me. This was to socialize them from the get-go. Sigi had never been left on her own, Melissa explained, and it showed. The way she nuzzled into my hand, it was obvious that she was completely comfortable with strangers. What also struck me was how piercing her eyes were – a dazzling azure blue. I almost melted when I looked into them. But then, Melissa spelled it out. 'She may be hard of hearing. We're not a hundred per cent sure yet. She's too young to know for sure, but it's something to be aware of,' she warned.

'Deaf?' I questioned. This was not something that had been on my radar at all and was not something Melissa had mentioned in our communication. I'd never even thought about how to cope with a deaf cat.

Melissa went on to explain how a very high percentage of white cats with blue eyes are deaf. By a roll of the genetic dice, the two are interlinked and more so if a cat is long-haired. If a white cat has a right eye that's blue, then it's likely to be deaf in that ear.

It's the same on the left side. Even if they are not born deaf, it's probable the cat's hearing will degrade over time.

I looked down at Sigi. Both of her eyes were bright blue. 'Okay, good of you to let me know,' I thanked Melissa, making a mental note that it was something we were going to have to keep a lookout for.

And it turned out Melissa was spot on. Over the next month, as I nursed Sigi in the spare room, I noticed that she didn't respond to any of my calls. To train her I'd bought a clicker – a small box with a metal tongue that I held in my hand and pressed right behind her ear so she could associate the sound with the reward of food.

Click. The snap of the box was loud, but Sigi didn't flinch once. She didn't even turn her head, even if I clicked right behind her ear. When I read up online, I started to understand how important vibration and movement is to deaf cats – tactile and visual clues to what's going on around them. *Maybe that was why she loved resting her paws against the steering wheel on the way home from Melissa's*, I wondered. Living with Sigi was going to be a learning curve for sure.

Periodically, I sent Melissa updates. I thanked her for warning me that Sigi may have special requirements and that as time went on she was probably right that Sigi was deaf. We were getting used to her quirks and finding ways around them. For instance, if I needed to attract Sigi's attention I would remind myself never to speak to her from behind, but to stand in front so she could make eye contact. If her food was ready I also made extra sure that she could feel my footsteps leading her to the kitchen, so she could sense the vibration along the floorboards and follow.

Whenever I wrote to Melissa I attached a photo or a video so she could see how Sigi was growing day by day, to reassure her that she'd placed her with a caring owner. But Melissa didn't reply. Weeks went by and even though I continued to send emails, there was never any answer. *That sucks,* I thought. She'd given the impression of being a super-nice woman and a very good breeder. I was surprised that she wasn't interested at all.

After a while, I got too curious and googled Melissa to see if she was still breeding cats or whether she'd given up. And that's when I saw her picture and the headline flash up:

HERMOSA BEACH COUPLE CONVICTED IN
FEDERAL TAX FRAUD CASE.

What the hell?

When I called Bianca in, we sat there in disbelief reading through court report after court report.

Melissa was no wine mom, it turned out. She and her husband David had been filing fraudulent tax documents for many years and embezzling millions of dollars in returns from the Internal Revenue Service. If that wasn't bad enough, David was a self-proclaimed psychic who went by the name of 'America's Prophet'. In the past, he'd made documentaries about the paranormal and spread conspiracy theories – the kind linked to far-right extremism in the States.

We counted back. On the day we picked Sigi up he had not

long been handed a six-year sentence in a federal prison. Judging by the timeline, Melissa would have been awaiting the start of her two-year sentence when we met. *Holy shit!*

I looked down at Sigi. She glanced up, her wide blue eyes almost pleading with me. 'Your breeders may be state felons, but they were damn good at raising great cats.' I smiled. That day it also dawned on me that maybe Sigi wasn't as straightforward as I'd imagined her to be.

3

THE THRILL OF
THE CHASE

Nobody could have predicted it, but by February 2020 the news had started spreading. At work, Ryan and I talked with endless fascination about the reports coming out of Central China – a trickle at first, before the wave got more intense. Video diaries of shoppers in the city of Wuhan dressed in white protective suits and masks loading groceries into trolleys from half-filled shelves started to dominate the headlines. Military-style lockdowns and streets lined with skyscrapers devoid of people and traffic looked eerily futuristic. The death toll had gone from one to a hundred and was now edging close to a thousand. Even so, a mystery virus only recently named Covid-19 by the World Health Organization felt very remote. This was something happening on the other side of the world and TV channels loved the drama, I thought. Ryan and I debated the chances of it spreading to London. Yeah, *maybe*, we concluded. But it didn't feel likely, whatever the forecasts. Besides, a full-on global pandemic was in the realms of science fiction, wasn't it?

In Belsize Park, anyhow, life could not have felt more normal. In the weeks since Christmas Bianca and I had established ourselves as fixtures in the neighbourhood, especially at the Steele. The guilt of not spending enough time with the cats had been partially solved. Ylva wouldn't have lasted two minutes in a crowded environment but every week I took Sigi out with me. Whereas in The Washington she curled up quietly on a cushion and watched the waitstaff sweep by juggling plates and glasses, in the Steele, she was treated like a regular who had already stolen a fair few hearts.

'Hey, it's Sigi!' Jazmin's voice raised several octaves whenever we stepped in, as if she were saying hi to a toddler. And, that's how the manager Stephen welcomed her too. A natural animal lover, he couldn't pass by our table without tickling Sigi under her chin or giving her head a friendly ruffle before collecting our empties and heading back to the bar. Without doubt, I noticed that having Sigi with us oiled the wheels of any relationship. Beforehand, we were a couple of Americans with strange accents, new in the area, who had found a friendly bar to drink in. But with our mascot Sigi we were gradually being elevated to local celebrity status.

Occasionally I took her to the pub quiz at the Steele, which happened every Wednesday night. Normally it would be only me and Bianca who formed our team. On other weeks we invited some of our more knowledgeable friends. Back home Bianca had done her bachelor's degree at the prestigious Massachusetts Institute of Technology and some of her fellow classmates had gravitated to London to work, just like us. Stephen loved the challenge of taking them down a peg or two.

'Was that MIT education *really* worth it?' he teased Bianca mercilessly as he chatted into his microphone to the crowd. It hadn't taken him long to work out that Bianca wasn't much good at pub trivia, and I turned out to be even worse. After we took a neuroscientist friend of hers there one time, Stephen took it as his cue to raise the stakes. The next Wednesday, when we all turned up together, he'd compiled a whole round on the brain and the body's nervous system. Much to his delight, we still didn't win. And of course, no music round, picture quiz or general knowledge round was complete without Stephen crowbarring in several questions on his own personal obsession – James Bond. You could hear the groans as we were forced to think about yet another obscure question on *The Spy Who Loved Me* or *Octopussy*. In the end, it became a running joke. All the while, Sigi sat patiently with us, blissfully unaware of the laughter and the music and the loud boom of Stephen talking. Having a deaf cat has its upsides, we realized.

At work too, Sigi had become a character, although in truth she had been ever since San Francisco. When I'd started working remotely, I'd set up a pet channel on our internal chat platform, Slack. I'd been part of a similar network when I was working in Silicon Valley and it had stuck with me – a fun way to break up the day and view something online that propelled programmers like me out of our mystifying world of whiteboard diagrams, data models and Python programming language. From the isolation of a study in the US, it also became a way to connect with colleagues around the world – a kind of universal language that reinforced our humanness despite our remote, high-tech lives, maybe even a digital stress reliever that forced people to think about something fun if only for random moments of their hectic days.

At first, there were around three of us posting pictures and videos of our pets. Initially I had posted up my collection of Sigi asleep on my keyboard and peeking out from behind the monitor and these had gone down well. Others posted their cats or dogs doing similarly silly things. And I do recall one colleague being the proud owner of a python snake. It didn't quite have the same fluffy appeal, but we appreciated that it meant something to him. Then, as word got round, followers of the channel grew. By the time I'd reached London, it had become popular with maybe a dozen or so colleagues all tuning in to post or comment on what updates people had uploaded. And in mid-February, it made sharing the drama of one particular day far more bearable.

Bianca and I had gotten up as usual. By then our furniture had arrived. We had a sofa, a desk and kitchen equipment and the flat had started to feel lived in and more like our own. As couples do, we'd fallen into our routine. Usually Bianca got up first, making breakfast and checking her emails before work. I followed, always more reluctant to start any day. That morning, I lay in bed making a mental checklist of the things I needed to do. Work had been flat out, establishing platforms with an increasing number of clients. If I didn't prioritize I'd drown. But it left little space for much else, especially not domestic duties. That said, if I didn't put a wash on soon, I'd run out of work clothes. In between my coffee and checking my emails I gathered up my pile of jeans and T-shirts from the bedroom and hurriedly loaded the washing machine.

It must have been around 9.30am when Bianca and I finally got ready to leave and like every morning I did my final check on the cats. Ylva was sound asleep in her basket, having already wolfed down her early morning breakfast. But Sigi was nowhere to be seen.

'Sigi, hey Sig!' It was my natural habit to call for Sigi, even though I knew she would never be able to hear. 'Have you seen Sigi?' I shouted to Bianca.

'Not since first thing,' she confirmed.

In the living room I checked around her favourite spots. There was a soft cushion that she loved to curl up on, but she wasn't there. I checked round the back of the sofa and underneath, but there was no sign of her there either. Nor was she in the bathroom or the kitchen or sat on her favourite ledge in the study, eyes glued to the cat superhighway. She wasn't even splayed out across the computer case under my desk soaking up its warmth like a sun worshipper on a California beach.

Just as I entered the hallway, my heart sank. *Shit*. I'd left the bedroom door open after I'd gone to fetch the washing. It was only ajar but it was enough for Sigi to slide through. An unfamiliar room to discover would be like catnip to her. As a rule we don't let the cats in the bedroom. Ylva has a habit of peeing on the bed every so often and neither of us want the task of cleaning the stench off our mattress. But there was a double whammy. Bianca and I sleep with the window slightly open.

'Bianca!' I shouted, panic now racing through me.

When I ran in, Sigi wasn't curled up on the bed. I threw back the sheets but she wasn't buried under them or hiding under the bed, or in the washing basket. I called again, but there was no sound and no miaow. When I got to the window, I could feel my pulse quicken. *Please be there,* I thought. I imagined her perched on the outside ledge huddling into the wall, having realized her mistake and waiting to be picked up and brought in.

But when I looked out, Sigi wasn't anywhere. I craned my head further and stared down at the 30-foot drop. If there's one thing Norwegian Forest cats are great at it's jumping – but within reason. Six foot is nothing to Sigi, around the height of the average fridge, and she can land with graceful precision like a ballerina perfecting her *grand jeté*. But 30 feet? I was struggling to see how that was possible. Could Sigi be that brave?

Bianca rushed in. Now both of us stood at the window our eyes combing over every patch of grass, every bush and every tree. I thought I saw a flash of white, but then realized it was only what I *wanted* to see. Most of all a terrible feeling of guilt crept through me. How could I have been so careless? Sigi was out there alone, unable to hear a thing.

'Let's split up. You search one half of the garden and I'll search the other,' I said to Bianca, pulling on my shoes.

It was freezing outside, but neither of us cared. By now we were frantic, on our hands and knees foraging under bushes, looking upwards along every branch of every tree. Surely a white cat would be obvious among the bare, black branches? We perched on our tiptoes and peered over fences into the neighbours' gardens, the mist of our breath visible against the February air. Nothing. As time ticked on, I wondered if we'd ever find Sigi. Surely she wasn't that desperate to escape?

At some point she'll want to come back to the warmth of her home?

'I can't go to work,' I announced, and Bianca agreed that she couldn't leave either. We couldn't rest until Sigi was found. By now, my mind was working overtime. The main road out front would be filled with cars at that time of the morning, exhausts belching on the return from the school run. Plus it was a bus route. But Sigi can't hear traffic or sense any danger whatsoever. What if she'd been hit and dumped like a twisted sack by the side of the road?

'I'll search while you call in and then we can swap,' Bianca said. I could see the anxiety in her eyes.

The call to work was more humiliating than anything else. Ringing in because you are vomiting your guts up and need to take time off is one thing. Taking a morning out for a lost cat that's *never* been outside on its own before only reflected back at me my own stupidity. Fortunately, the news was met with kind concern and good humour. 'I'll be in as soon as I can,' I told Ryan.

'Sure man. Keep us updated,' he said, knowing how dedicated I was to my cats. Besides, a real live feline drama unfolding on Slack could make the hours fly by. I was about to hang up when I heard a breathless Bianca pounding up the stairwell.

'Travis! Travis! I've seen her. Come quickly,' she hollered before running back down.

Fantastic! I thought. Drama over. But when I finally made it to the front porch Bianca was further down the pathway peering up the road.

'She's just gone past. I saw her! But she's gone,' she said, shrugging frustratedly. Apparently, just as Bianca stepped out she'd caught a flash of ginger tom speeding past the open gate, followed by a messy bundle of white galloping behind. But now, they'd disappeared. Yup. It all made sense. The ginger tom was another local resident and a regular on the cat superhighway. For weeks it had been coolly strolling by, practically flipping the bird at Sigi each and every time. Clearly Sigi had been bottling up all her anger for the moment when she could escape and the two of them could fight it out feline to feline. *Whatever state she was in now, at least she's alive*, I smiled.

In my pocket I felt my phone buzz. A client needed some information ready for a service launch that week. I'd have to juggle Operation Sigi with some delegation. I called the team and then posted an update on Slack: *No cat news yet, but things looking more pawsitive*. It felt like it was time for a little laughter, but I could hear the groans already.

For the next hour or so Bianca and I searched up and down the street constantly retracing our steps. I rang the doorbell of the house next door, but no one answered. The woman two doors down hadn't seen anything, and Mary upstairs said she'd keep a lookout and wished us luck. Bianca had already searched under every parked car and was contemplating a search of the neighbours' trash bins. I'd also been out on to the main road and looked up and down the gutters, terrified of what I might find. As I predicted, the road was bumper to bumper traffic, but among it all there was no Sigi.

When I glanced over to the other side of the street several people were sat sipping their morning coffees in the windows of the cafes. Some were alone staring out at the world going by. Surely, they'd have spotted her?

'Excuse me. Have you seen a cat? White? Maybe a bit angry?' I asked.

'Sorry mate.' The answer was the same from everyone.

It felt like we were back to square one, but as Bianca and I were regrouping outside of our block, we heard a sudden shout. An elderly neighbour was making her way down the street. 'Hello! Hello!' She had her hand raised up trying to catch our attention. 'You're the young man with the white cat, aren't you?' she called as she got closer.

'Yes!' I replied, searching her eyes for any hopeful sign. A smile broke from the corner of her mouth.

'It's right there,' she laughed, pointing upwards at a tree facing our row, a few houses down. The woman had seen us trawling up and down the pavement and put two and two together.

I fixed my eyes on the tree and slowly worked my way up its trunk, then it's branches. I raised my head further. Around 70 feet up, balancing precariously between the trunk and a large branch, was Sigi, fur so messed up that she looked like a cross between Albert Einstein and a sheepskin rug. She was sat deadly still and staring at us.

'Thank God!' I said, before thanking the woman repeatedly, but when I turned to Bianca she was giggling nervously.

'Great! But how the hell are we going to get her down?' she asked. I had no idea. Stage two of Operation Sigi was about to commence.

By now, my co-workers were demanding updates: *Found!*

I posted on the Slack channel. I suspect some colleagues found it sweet that we were so worried. In a land where cats roam free, why worry about one stuck up a tree? But there were lots of laughter emojis sent to me too. I even got my telescope out and attached my phone camera to it so I could get a close-up shot that I could post. Sigi did not look amused by my paparazzi impression. My guess was that either the ginger tom had raced up first but had managed to find its way back down; or maybe a more likely explanation was that Sigi had lost interest and got distracted by a squirrel sprinting up the oak tree.

'Let's go in and wait by the window until she makes it down,' I suggested. Where Sigi was positioned was far too high for me to climb. Besides, at some point she'd get cold or hungry, I figured. It was bitter, overcast and damp, and I didn't want to be outside. But Bianca wasn't listening to that.

'She's alone. We have to stay with her,' she demanded.

The problem is, the depths of a British winter mean nothing to a Norwegian Forest cat. Beneath her glossy overcoat Sigi is insulated with a woolly undercoat, perfectly adapted for sub-zero temperatures. We could be out there for the long haul.

'Okay, okay,' I replied, but I was going to need extra layers. And if were out there for the duration, we were going to have to devise some way of coaxing her down. Minutes later I appeared with some dry treats in a plastic container which I shook at her.

'Hey Sig, you must be hungry, huh?'

She glanced down dismissively. She could not have looked less interested. The winds of the last few days had eased off, so there was nothing budging her and there was great birdwatching to be done from up there. Plus, she would have had spectacular views across the entire city. Nearby Primrose Hill is one of the best spots to enjoy London's awesome skyline. From that vantage point, you can see landmarks like the BT Tower, the London Eye, the Shard and the skyscrapers of London's financial district rising majestically from the trees.

A couple of hours passed by. By now I was bouncing between urgent work emails and checking back on Sigi. Bianca was camped out on the steps shivering but still refusing to come inside. Then, at around midday, we looked up. One spot first, then a couple more flecks, then a smattering of rain. I smiled. If there's one thing Sigi hates it's rain. Still perched between the branches, her ears were now pointed bolt upright and she was shaking her head frantically. Every miaow became louder and deeper. *Only a matter of time now,* I thought.

Sure enough, as the drops got heavier Sigi became restless, wriggling around on the branch and attempting to back herself out. Then, we watched in astonishment as she skilfully made her way across one branch, as if she were a high-wire circus act. One paw stepped cautiously in front of the other, careful to get the balance spot on. From there she continued on to the branch of an adjacent oak, but sadly the flawless performance ended there. From then on her descent became one of the clumsiest manoeuvres I had ever seen. With their muscular bodies and thick, sharp claws, Norwegian Forest cats are fantastic at climbing, but not so clever at coming down. Around halfway she gripped the bark, trying to cling on. And at around 10 feet from the ground, it was obvious she was losing grip.

'Hang on Sig,' I shouted, running to catch her, but when she took a final tumble, my outstretched arms weren't best positioned to carry her full weight. She rolled from my hands and crashed down untidily in a rain-soaked bush, flipping over like a stunt car.

'Hey Sigi. You okay?' I said, quickly scooping her out. She was clearly rattled by the whole experience so I held her into my chest and gave her the biggest cuddle ever. She was covered in mud and small broken branches were matted in her fur. When we took her inside, we warmed her with a blanket in the kitchen before gently washing her in warm water. And afterwards it was the only time we let her curl up on our bed. She passed out so quickly and twitched in the deepest sleep as Bianca and I lay on either side of her stroking her to keep her calm. I imagined she was still thinking about that ginger tom and how he'd got away.

A couple of days later at work, Sigi even made the headlines in the weekly all-staff meeting. A colleague had mocked up a slide with two pictures I'd posted on the Slack channel: one of Sigi up the tree and the other of her in our kitchen looking stunned and dishevelled. Underneath, she'd written the words *CATastrophe averted. Department of Feline Rescue. Travis saved his cat.* When I looked around, everyone's faces were glued to the large screen and the room erupted with laughter. As it did, a warm, satisfied feeling spread through me. For the first time in a very long time I realized I felt part of a team. Part of something good.

4

CALIFORNIA CALLING

Maybe I've always been a bit of loner. I was born in 1975 in
Longview, Washington State, on the banks of the mighty
Columbia River. Once a stop on the only route from Canada
to New Mexico, it sits within a vast landscape flanked by
snow-peaked mountains and billowing volcanoes. The wide
river basin winds from the Pacific Northwest all the way up to
British Columbia. And to cross at Longview you have to take
the Lewis and Clark Bridge which dominates the city – its heavy
steel construction built in the 1930s to support the state's then
flourishing timber industry. All that space, yet growing up there
felt narrow and claustrophobic.

My parents separated before I have any memory of them
living together. My earliest memories are of my mum Tami
and her boyfriend David, the man she went on to marry. An
impatient man and a hard drinker, I never thought of him as a
stepfather, or any kind of father. That said, I never thought of
my own father, Dennis, as much of a presence in my life either.

Now, I think it's probably important for boys to have stable role models, but my family were anything but. As far as I was concerned, I was more of an afterthought than born from a burning desire to have kids.

My dad didn't have a regular profession. As I later understood, when he and my mother split and he moved to Snohomish County near Seattle, he was a part-time carpenter. We kept in touch, and when my mum and David moved from Longview to Molalla in Oregon, I used to get taken there every weekend to his place, which was surrounded by forest. He'd since remarried and he and his new wife lived with my half-brother Greg and half-sister Ashley. I can't say I enjoyed visiting much. Dad was a man's man. A guy who wouldn't look out of place on the set of the Peter Fonda classic *Easy Rider*: all wide-brimmed Stetson, bushy moustache and heavy stubble.

I'll never forget when I was around 12 that he bought me an 80cc Honda dirt bike so I could ride out through the forest clearings. A boy's rite of passage would have been his reasoning, but I was terrified. 'Just handle yourself, son! What are you whining about? No one's capable if they can't ride a bike,' he said after I stood there hesitant to hop on and rev up the engine. Being 'capable' was very important to my dad. He had that boomer mentality that if you didn't automatically know how to do stuff or build stuff then you weren't a real man. At other times he'd wrestle me to the ground and hold me there in a headlock until I burst into tears, trying to build me up to be the tough guy he probably sensed I was never going to be.

But my father also disappeared every year for months on

end. The Gulf of Alaska was the place where men temporarily migrated to in order to earn enough money for the whole year, and many like him from the cities of Seattle and Portland did. There, king salmon season runs from May to August, and he'd take a trawler out with his fellow fishermen and catch fish for weeks. Seasons spent outside hauling in nets and shovelling salmon on deck had weathered his hands and face, and violent storms often threatened the safety of the crew. Once I remember him arriving home with a tall tale of a walrus that his boat hit not long after they'd sailed out from the harbour. Its dead weight destabilized the vessel and as it began sinking he was forced to dive into the icy water and swim to shore with the waves crashing around him.

Years later, when my half-brother Greg reached his teens, he joined him for a season but came home swearing he'd never do it again. Living on a cramped boat with fishermen doing back-breaking work was way too much for him. Besides, once proper commercial fishing started in the region, it became harder for men to make a decent living.

'Those damn Japanese,' I always heard my father say after boats began arriving, fishing for greater quantities of salmon and undercutting the price of fish to the extent that men like him could only eek a living. Nevertheless, he continued fishing the salmon season right up until his sixties when he retired.

What I did inherit from my father was an ability to turn my hand to almost any do-it-yourself job. Right beside his home he had a small workshop where he kept all his carpentry and mechanics tools, and I used to spend hours rummaging through screwdrivers and saws and running my fingers across the try squares and Stanley knives. When I moved to San Francisco I had a garage below our apartment that didn't look dissimilar. I even bought a red tool box identical to his to remind myself of the pleasure of discovering his workshop. In fact, over the years I lived in the Sunset District, I taught myself how to restore a beautiful classic 1963 Chevy II Nova car. Through following online tutorials in my spare time, I learned how to change its engine and replace the transmission and rebuild it until it was good enough to drive.

And later, in the summer of 2017 after Sigrid arrived, I built her the most powerful fan you could imagine. That year was the hottest on record and a searing 106°F heat stifled the city – unbearable for a cat covered in thick hair. As the sun streamed in through our windows, Sigi refused to move from her cushion. Every time I petted her she looked despondent, her eyes drooped and she drifted back to sleep. In the end, she also stopped eating. We got so worried that we took her to the vet, who confirmed she was suffering from heatstroke and sent us home with instructions to hydrate her regularly with a bone-based broth administered through a syringe, which also boosted her calories.

'Here, open wide Sigi,' I said, forcing her jaw open while Bianca plunged the barrel. Not a pleasant experience for any of us but one that was necessary. But our heat trap of an apartment only got hotter and Sigi more miserable. And that's when I had the idea: a couple of spare radiator fans had been kicking around my garage for months – the size of a car wheel and the kind of voltage a racing car might use. So I mounted them on a large wooden frame and sat them in the living room connected to the mains. Sigi didn't hang back for a moment. Switched on, the fans were powerful enough to slam shut every door in the apartment, but Sigi blissed out in front of them for hours: head raised, eyes closed and her hair blowing back like she was driving a convertible along the windy California coast. Even now in London, she can while away hours in the summer sitting on top of the air filter in the study, or she'll head for the pavement vents above the London Underground and rest there until I tug her leash signalling it's time to go.

My early life was similarly do-it-yourself, but not in such a positive way. School had not been on my mum's radar for me at all. Just like my dad, she barely held down a succession of insecure jobs, from working as a hotel receptionist for a short while to selling car seats in a sheepskin shop. Her biggest boast was that she'd once served Arnold Schwarzenegger, who'd rolled into town on a body-building tour. I was what you'd call a latchkey kid. When I woke up, Mum would be gone and when I came home, she'd still be gone.

Nothing much was expected of me academically. Any aspirations I had got stamped on quickly. 'You'll never be smart enough to go to college,' Mum told me. In fact, she often described me as 'annoying'. If I got something into my head, I'd go for it full throttle, like the time when I was around ten and I rearranged my toy cupboard, thinking it would make her happy.

'What are you doing Travis? Why is this on the floor?' I can still hear her shouting when she found me in my room surrounded by neat piles of toys. The body blow felt unbearable. I had done it to please her, but I was being far too ambitious, she said and ordered me to clear the mess immediately.

I suspect that's one of the reasons why I found it hard to focus as I progressed through school. All my grand ideas would dissolve and I probably talked myself into being an underachiever, scared of how any success might play out back home. It didn't help that in elementary school I'd been picked out for a talented and gifted students programme. I scored a high IQ – around 156 – but I never seemed able to sustain anything, nor was I given much support. Smart clothes for school and school supplies were always provided to me by my mum but there was zero chance of her ever sending me to a good school. My parents hadn't gone on to college themselves and there was no expectation that I would break the mould.

Long-lasting friendships had also been difficult to develop. My mum's and David's unstable incomes meant that we moved at the drop of a hat. From Molalla we packed up and moved to a prefab trailer home in Colton, a rural logging town where there was also a pistol and rifle factory. And from there, we headed back to Washington State to near Stevenson. For me that was the worse move, in part because it was all so sudden.

One afternoon, Mum turned up at school. 'Travis, can you go to the principal's office please,' the teacher said, pulling me out of class.

When I approached the office Mum was waiting at reception.

'You won't be coming back,' she announced as we headed out towards her car.

It was so confusing. 'Why? What's happening? Where are we going?' I pleaded.

'David and I have bought a house. We're going back to Washington State,' she told me matter-of-factly, with no explanation whatsoever. All my belongings had been piled into the boot packed in bags and suitcases, and Mum and David only ever returned to Colton once to empty the rest of the house. There was no chance to say goodbye to friends. Instead, that day we headed north, stayed overnight at a motel and continued our journey the next morning. Years later I found out that the rumour buzzing around school was that I'd died. One day I was in class, the next day I wasn't. For 14-year-olds it would have been a credible explanation.

My one saving grace were my grandparents. Both my paternal and maternal grandparents had mainly stayed in Washington State and during the summer holidays I would often get sent to stay with them, mainly to my mum's mother's house. When I think about her and her second husband Bob now, I suspect they understood that I was not a well-looked-after kid but both my grandmothers spoiled me with toys and gifts.

The weatherboard house we ended up in near Stevenson had been secured by my mother's father. A logger by trade, he also bought up tracts of forest land, cleared it, sold the trees and built on it, or restored dilapidated houses before selling them on for profit. By this time the logging industry was in steep decline and unemployment was rising – once thriving communities left unskilled and destitute not unlike when the coal mines in the UK closed during the 1980s, ripping the heart out of towns and leaving nothing in their place but workless men and families plunged into poverty. As I recall, some people were barely surviving. Hard liquor and crystal meth spread like a cancer through godforsaken towns and in the Native American reservations that also punctuated the landscape, poverty was even more acute.

The problem for me was that our one-bedroom house, located off a two-lane highway overlooking the Columbia River, didn't have any neighbours, and with no other kids to interact with a feeling of isolation took hold. Now I think of the surrounding acres of Douglas firs as idyllic countryside. And, having lived in cities for so long, I appreciate the healing nature of America's outland, or 'God's Country' as my grandfather was so fond of calling it. But as a 14-year-old boy the enforced isolation in a drizzly backwater made the relocation a very difficult transition for me.

I was embarking on my freshman year, but now school was over an hour away by bus. When I arrived home I was unable to go anywhere. The nearest store, which was a run-down gas station, was 1 mile away. My nearest schoolfriend lived 6 miles from our house and by the early evening all Mum and David wanted to do was watch TV. If there was ever a school dance or friends wanted to hang out in town I could rarely join them. All the first kisses and clumsy socializing that teenagers do were off-limits to me.

And if David did ever agree to drive me it would be a 50-mile round trip, which he'd often do with a tumbler of his favourite drink placed on the mat by the clutch pedal. He'd periodically bend down to sip from it, one hand still resting on the wheel. 'I can't believe you made me come out here and pick you up,' he constantly complained, and one time when he turned a corner too hard and the glass tipped over all hell broke loose. Probably, I was quietly pleased David's precious drink got spilled, but after a while I became too scared to ask to be taken anywhere knowing the arguments it could spark. Instead, my attic room that had been loosely converted became my safe haven. And thanks to my maternal grandmother Carole I discovered computers and, soon, the internet.

Looking back, I reckon my grandmother was way ahead of her time especially given the traditional culture she existed in – she was what you might call an early adopter. She worked as a secretary and because of that she'd been one of the very few people to own a PC which she used for word-processing. Of course, it was nothing like the sleek desktops or laptops we use today. Instead, her Apple computer weighed a ton and looked more like a clunky old portable TV.

In the summers when I stayed with her she taught me how to log on and type, and she even had in her collection some of the initial text-based computer games like *The Hitchhiker's Guide to the Galaxy* and *Zork*, which she installed for me to play. Simply by typing in commands, I found myself transported to imaginary worlds, hunting through the ruins of the Great Underground Empire, moving from room to room and overcoming obstacles to uncover hidden treasure. Unlike at school, where I was failing, it felt like I was accomplishing something. With hours to spend on my own, I also taught myself very basic programming. By then I had my own Apple computer which my grandmother replaced with a Commodore 64. And later I worked from a PC which I built myself from various computer parts. Many of the initial text-based games came with a source code which I could easily input, and games magazines also printed the source codes which I messed around with to modify each game.

The timing could not have been better. Around the time when we moved back to Washington State it was at the cusp of the internet revolution – not that technology ever reached the Pacific Northwest too fast. However, in North Bonneville, a city about 12 miles away, there was one guy running a hyperlocal bulletin board that had about five members. This was pre-internet when a handful of people could log on with a username and password and dial into each other's PCs – small, virtual communities springing up across America and the forerunners of today's vast social media networks. Dialling in took for ever. The beeps and screeches of the modem became the hallmark sounds of a new digital age bridging the analogue divide. I could spend hours in front of the screen chatting and playing with people I'd never met. And it was cheap to use because I was only ever dialling in local area codes.

But as soon as I discovered America Online, the bills started racking up. Better known as AOL, the company has now fallen into relative obscurity, but then it was the first countrywide service provider in the States. Free floppy discs flooded through people's letter boxes that you could install if you wanted to join. Then, when CD-ROMs took over, new users could upload these to their hard drives, input their payment details and access AOL's growing community of users. Chat rooms and games dominated the service and there was even a first iteration of instant messaging. I was hooked.

Thankfully, it was one expense that my mum didn't care about. The $300 monthly phone bills were worth it to her so I could stay in my room. While her and David sat downstairs undisturbed I was discovering role-playing games like *Neverwinter Nights*, set in the fantasy world of Dungeons & Dragons. Incredible to think it was the first online multiplayer game that featured graphics, albeit very elementary. Every character I played felt like a better, more exciting version of myself – pure escapism from the hellhole I found myself in. And no one ever died in those games. Even after combat, there was a way to redeem your character and be brought back to life.

I also recall that early internet culture being so different from today's. I was a 14-year-old kid who thought nothing of chatting to another kid from Indiana, or a 50-year-old housewife from Iowa. No one ever knew who anyone was. No one knew whether the person you chatted to or played games with used their real name or an alias – it didn't matter. Social media profiles didn't exist but neither did some of the toxicity of today's online world. Nothing ever felt threatening or unusual about being a teenager online.

As I continued through college, teachers suggested that instead of completing my final year at high school I should attend a community college. It ran a programme called Running Start that was designed for gifted kids, but ones who were struggling in class. The upside was that the college ran computer courses, the one subject I could excel in. While the state paid for my first year, if I'd wanted to carry on I would have to fund it myself. Yet again education ended up being a stop–start process for me. My parents paying for classes was never an option. As far as Mum and David were concerned, any future job in computing was an absurd concept. Boys graduating from the kinds of run-down schools I attended mainly did one of two jobs: they entered the logging industry or they joined the military. As soon as I turned 16, David even set me up with work as a choker setter – the guy sent running down hills to wrap chains around falling logs so they can be pulled up by the heavy logging skidders. Lopped-off fingers or feet or broken ankles were seen as just occupational hazards.

As far as the military went, it was a route I had seriously considered. Army recruiters frequently toured economically depressed communities like ours and they were regulars at our school. Such was the dysfunction of my home life that there was something attractive about its regimentation and not having to take responsibility for my everyday living. I could simply turn up and have someone tell me what to do. Besides, I also leaned into hard physical exercise – sport was something I'd always enjoyed – and signing up would have the added advantage of getting me away from the house.

Part of the appeal was that neither my real father nor David had ever sat me down and taught me anything about how to care for myself as a man. In fact, they taught me nothing about my well-being at all. I'd even got into trouble the first time I shaved.

I must have been around 15 when I took one of David's disposable razors from the bathroom cabinet and dragged it across my dry skin leaving my cheeks red raw. No one had told me that I needed soap and water to build up a lather first. But David didn't care about that. All he was bothered about was that I'd stolen his razor without asking. My fingernails were left to grow long too. I bit them down constantly, until a classmate suggested to me that maybe I should use a set of clippers. I had no idea what that was.

Yet there was also a stubborn part of me that was determined to get a formal education regardless of the limited horizons my family had mapped out for me. Then fate stepped in. Around 1994 when I was 18 and I'd been on the Running Start programme for a while, one teacher noticed my computer knowledge was way ahead of the class. He gave me a textbook that accompanied a course he was teaching and, after that, invited me to assist him to teach other students struggling to pass their exams. I loved the extra work, even though I wasn't being paid to do it. Sharing my home-grown expertise with students who may otherwise fail felt so satisfying. For once, my knowledge was being appreciated. And it was through him that I met a guy who was to set up the first internet provider in the county.

Bryan was another early adopter – a quiet, focused guy but a smart entrepreneur at a time when the internet was far more makeshift and less cemented in Silicon Valley. Bryan also didn't care that I hadn't gone to university and didn't have any higher qualifications. If I could handle any work he passed to me then that was fine by him. Small jobs dripped in fairly regularly: maybe some basic programming work or he'd call me if an office needed some computers installed or an email server set up. By then I had my first car – a V W Dasher (known as the Passat in the UK). Later I would replace it with a Honda Prelude. But these weren't simply cars to me: they represented freedom. Driving meant I could work for him when, and if, he asked. For the first time in years I wasn't confined to my attic room.

With wheels I was also discovering a social life and travelling with friends to festivals and concerts. The band Nirvana had broken through on the Billboard charts and with singer Kurt Cobain and bassist Krist Novoselic growing up in Aberdeen, a similarly depressed logging city south of Seattle, I felt a natural affinity with the grunge scene and dressed in the same baggy jeans and check flannel shirts. I even saw Nirvana play a benefit gig at Portland Meadows in 1992 after the album *Nevermind* was released and they'd been elevated to the biggest rock band in the world. Two years later when Kurt Cobain shot himself, the shock waves reverberated through us. It was such a violent death of a true pioneer of the movement.

With the pockets of money I was earning, I also tried to pay for extra qualifications at college, and though I managed to complete several modules over the next few years I could never finance myself long enough to carry on to a degree. I also applied for basic programming work elsewhere but never heard back. At home, I continued to make friends online. Through AOL I'd progressed from being a dedicated gamer to helping run a multiplayer game. These old-school precursors to today's PC games were called MUDs and I ran a game called *SneezyMUD* – another version of a Dungeons & Dragons fantasy, but unlike *Neverwinter Nights* it had no graphics. I had got friendly online with its developer Russ, and we teased each other. The game often had bugs in it or the administrators had built in new features that we all moaned about.

Hey, I can help you fix a bunch of stuff, I messaged him.

Think you can do better? he joked, but from thereon in he brought me on board. Once I'd worked out the spaghetti of code, I could modify games, add features and build extra levels as well as continue to play.

Another guy, Rob, who I also talked to regularly, was a gamer who lived in San Francisco. He and I were often online at the same time and we discovered a mutual like of industrial music and hip hop. *How come you have so much time to play?* he asked me one day. I told him about the work I'd been doing for Bryan but that it was impossible to find full-time employment where I lived, even though I had the skills.

A few months down the line, he messaged me. *Hey man. There's a position going at my company. You should apply.* I was taken aback. A proper interview with a tech firm was an opportunity I hadn't expected, though I imagined Mum's and David's relief if I did announce I was moving to another state entirely. I was now in my early twenties and living at home continued to be unbearable, more so because I was a young man desperate for my independence yet I felt so trapped by my circumstances. Mum and David had also already tried to charge me rent, probably to encourage me to move out anyway, but with work being so irregular and juggling paid-for education courses, I'd been unable to pay.

Sure, I replied to Rob.

The job was in Palo Alto, a city overlooking the Bay Area on the road to San Jose. If I got it, I'd be working for a biotech company that had been mapping the human genome. It wasn't my area of knowledge, but that didn't matter. The company needed someone with basic programming skills to manage data and write sequencing software. I breezed through my first interview by phone, and for the second interview got flown to California to hang out with the team. To me, the proposed salary of $45,000 was mind-blowing. However, it wasn't long before I realized that that was peanuts compared to the megabucks programmers could earn in Silicon Valley.

Nevertheless, when the job was offered to me, I accepted immediately. At last a route out of Washington State that would make the last few years of free tutoring and odd jobs with Bryan worthwhile: a job where my mainly self-taught skills would be of value. Another part of me also wanted to show my family that I was making something of my life: that I was 'capable' – that word that my dad had drummed into me. And maybe prove to my mum that I was right to stick at college all that time and want more from life than a logging job or the military.

The day I packed up my car to leave, David did the weirdest, but probably most generous, thing he'd done throughout our entire relationship. 'Here, you'll need these,' he said, running across the driveway to hand me a plate, bowl, cup and cutlery all neatly wrapped in a tea towel.

'It's fine. I'll grab some at Walmart,' I refused, before jumping in the car and heading south. At age 23 I was finally free.

5

LOCKDOWN

By early March 2020, Covid-19 was spreading and fast. It was only a matter of time before the scenes playing out in other European cities would happen in the UK. Italy looked dire. Every morning I checked my Twitter feed and looked through reports coming out of the northern region of Lombardy: nurses dressed head to toe in blue protective suits and heavy masks. It felt surreal, as were the grisly details of the virus itself: people gasping for breath; people hooked up to respirators; patients being wheeled in bio-containers normally seen on the sets of sci-fi movies; and the numbers of people dying doubling every day. Italy went into a national lockdown in early March, with bars and restaurants closed and travel to and from the country halted. It was the same story in Spain and France. Yet despite what I was seeing and reading online, it still felt like the credits would roll and the movie would end.

By comparison, there had been a handful of confirmed deaths from Covid in the UK – around 50. Infection rates were

multiplying, though, and there was a quiet unease at work, but
mainly life carried on. Bianca and I had even started discovering
some of the places we wanted to see outside London. Oxford had
been on our radar and we visited on one of our free weekends.
I'd already been on a previous work trip there and had fallen
for the city's spires and its ancient past stretching back to the
Neolithic Age. As much as Americans try, we can't beat England
on history and I wanted Bianca to enjoy it, too. Alongside some
art-hopping, we took in the weird and wonderful exhibits at the
Pitt Rivers Museum: the most random collection of artefacts
I'd ever seen. From jewellery to clothing, armoury and art, the
collection was gathered from British colonies around the world.
Frankly, its shrunken heads and human remains freaked us both
out. So much so, that when we left we needed to unwind over a
few beers at The Eagle and Child pub on St Giles' – a beautiful
wood-panelled bar and another famous landmark to tick off
my list. Having immersed myself in fantasy and role play as a
teenager, the pub where the authors J R R Tolkien and C S Lewis
had famously spent evenings debating held a very special appeal.

Back in London, we gravitated over winter towards the
kind of nightlife we'd enjoyed in San Francisco in areas like the
Castro. Otherwise known as the Gayborhood, it's the place
where LGBTQ+ flags fly proudly and even the zebra crossings
are painted over with the colours of the rainbow. Being a fan of
RuPaul's Drag Race, Bianca was keen to visit the Royal Vauxhall
Tavern – a historic London pub south of the River Thames
famous for its drag queens and gay cabaret. To be honest, drag
isn't really my thing. Mostly, I loved the comedy nights put on by

a performance group called The Cocoa Butter Club who we saw on stage in Dalston. A show bursting with laughter turned out to be the best pick-me-up on a cold February night, alongside our usual Wednesday night pub quiz at the Steele.

Thinking further afield, we'd also booked tickets for a festival in April. Bianca and I were both due a long weekend and craft beer company BrewDog had announced its annual beer-fuelled blowout in Aberdeen. I'd also heard that the East Coast Main Line from London King's Cross Station through York and the Scottish Borders is spectacular, winding its way up through Edinburgh and along Scotland's rugged coastline until it reaches the north. I'd only visited Scotland once before, so it was one adventure we were counting on.

But as March pushed on, those plans looked more in doubt. By then the trickle of Covid-19 deaths had mushroomed. Apparently earlier numbers had been underestimated due to a time lag in reporting deaths. Infections continued soaring. I researched further online, this time bypassing the mainstream news and heading straight to Google Scholar. Never mind what the British government were telling the public: according to Prime Minister Boris Johnson the pandemic would turn the tide in twelve weeks, but I didn't believe that. When I began to scan through the scientific papers and their predictions, the prognosis didn't look so rosy.

By mid-month we debated using the theatre tickets we had bought for a play in the West End called *The Seagull* – an adaptation of Chekhov that had received rave reviews and featured a favourite *Game of Thrones* actor Emilia Clarke. With talk of a lockdown growing, we figured it might get cancelled, but when it wasn't, we agreed to enjoy what we thought may be our last night out for a while. I felt an odd mixture of emotions. So far, I'd experienced nothing but warmth from Londoners, but as soon as we got there I noticed an underlying suspicion and anxiety creeping in. The theatre was sold out, but a handful of people sat wearing disposable masks which immediately struck me as alien and impersonal.

'How many people here have it and don't know?' I whispered to Bianca, looking round the faces in the auditorium before the lights went down.

'You can't worry about it Travis.' She shrugged, but I could also sense her concern. Interval drinks became an obstacle course of avoidance as Bianca and I hung out in a far corner of the foyer not wanting to manoeuvre too close to other guests. The black cab home felt equally as strange. We sat unmasked with the windows open an inch or so. As the car weaved through Central London, I saw pockets of partygoers spilling out on to the pavement shouting and hugging each other drunkenly as if nothing was happening. It bothered me. *Don't people understand how serious this could be?* I thought. Or maybe they just don't care?

At the beginning of the next week the measures that everyone had been expecting were confirmed. Restaurants, bars, theatres and leisure centres would close, as would most shops other than those selling essentials. At work, we got pulled into an all-staff meeting, and I recall the wall of silence that initially greeted our founder, Brandon. Many of our clients came from the retail and hospitality sectors – the exact same sectors now forced to shut up shop.

Brandon took a deep breath. 'I'm sorry guys. We've made the difficult decision to close the office,' he announced to everyone piled into the room. I could feel my stomach knot. I'd only just arrived and my work visa was specifically linked to this job. Besides, travel was shutting down. A ban on travel from the UK to the US had not long been put in place. Where could we go? As I stood there, it felt as though the floor was about to be pulled from underneath me. 'We'll get the systems fully set up so that every department can work from home,' he continued.

Immediately, I could feel the unease in the room lift, as did mine. No jobs were being lost; people were still going to get paid. *Thank God. The one great thing about working for a tech company*, I thought – at least the transition to homeworking would feel seamless. After all, most of us already worked, or had previously worked, flexibly and others dialled in from around the world.

What didn't feel as seamless was my own internal transition. Bianca and I had only just started building a new life and finding friends in a foreign country. Sigi and Ylva were happy at home too. That evening, as I stepped off the 168 bus on Haverstock Hill, one of the first things I noticed were the lights out in the Steele. It looked eerily empty and a sadness washed over me. We hadn't even had chance to talk to Stephen or Jazmin and say how sorry we were that we wouldn't see them, or for them to give Sigi one last tickle before they closed down the bar. Out of curiosity, I also took a detour down England's Lane. The Washington had a note pinned to its door telling regulars it had also temporarily closed but that the owners hoped to be able to open the pub again soon. As I climbed our stairs a strange dislocation hit me, as if my brain and body were separate entities.

'Hey there,' I greeted Sigi as I opened the door. It was a comfort to see her – a part of my life that now felt reassuringly constant. She'd been waiting in the hallway and when I slumped down on the sofa she hopped up and plonked herself on my chest purring loudly – Sigi-speak for *I want attention now!* I hugged her tightly, showering her head with kisses before she curled up and slept there for much of the evening and I closed my eyes to the drone of the TV. At times Sigi was so rested that she began drooling. When I looked down and ran my fingers though her soft hair, I felt a bizarre envy of her. Sigi didn't have to worry about work or paying bills or about how she was going to get through this unsettling time. How amazing it must be to be so unaware of any responsibility or danger. No anxiety. No pressure. Just a loving family and a warm home to enjoy.

The next morning Bianca and I began planning. As well as washing our hands regularly as the public service announcements advised, she wanted to pick up a supply of hand sanitizer. We shared a hallway with other people and while we didn't want to catch coronavirus, we also didn't want to spread it. We didn't have disposable masks either, but I did have a temporary solution. When we'd shipped our belongings I'd included the majority of tools from my garage. In one box I'd packed masks in case I needed to fix something in the flat or weld any metal together. Back in the States I'd made the odd piece of jewellery and crafted items like iron candle holders and I'd found the hobby relaxing. I brought one mask out and strapped it on.

Bianca could not stop laughing. 'Oh my God, Travis. It's like you're stepping out in a nuclear holocaust!'

The mask didn't cover my eyes, but it did cover my nose and mouth and it was heavy-duty enough with its side filters to look like a wartime respirator. In fact, we'd first bought them in Reno – a miniature Las Vegas – the year that Sigi arrived. On our way back from a friend's wedding, the road up ahead had become barely navigable. Given the soaring temperatures, the California wildfires were raging. Thick smoke billowed up from the surrounding forestland and we'd got caught. Californians expect fires every summer but that year they'd become so intense that the Bay Area turned a ghostly orange and ash clouds obscured the two towers of the Golden Gate Bridge. That day we'd stopped by a gas station, picked a couple of masks up, closed the car windows and battled home. Sigi and I didn't take our regular walks out for days.

On a leafy street in North London, though, I looked like I was fresh from cooking up crystal meth in the TV drama *Breaking Bad*. All I needed was a hazmat suit. As I zipped up my motorbike jacket, I noticed from the corner of my eye Sigi staring up at me quizzically, like the newest recruit to the fashion police. *Holy shit, he's going out dressed like that?* I could hear her say.

'Yep, Sigi. It's the new normal. Wish me luck!' I smiled as I headed out. In truth, I felt achingly self-conscious. Being very early days, the production and wearing of masks hadn't ramped up. Some people were protected, others weren't. By the time I reached the corner store a few hundred metres down the street, the number of people staring had begun to rattle me. Then one woman approached, waving her hand to grab my attention.

'Excuse me.' She was young with wide eyes and her face looked vaguely familiar, but I couldn't place her. I stopped, slightly taken aback. Maybe she was going to tell me I looked too nightmarish for Belsize Park?

'Mmhum,' I tried to answer, forgetting that my mouth was covered.

'Where do you get one of those?' she asked, squinting up at me.

This time, I lifted up the rubber mouthpiece to explain.

'I know how bad those wildfires get in California!' she bubbled enthusiastically. It was as if she was happy to have made the connection and we ended up chatting for a while.

'Maybe you can find one online,' I suggested before heading off.

'Thanks. I'm Laura, by the way. Laura Pradelska.'

'Travis,' I said, holding out my hand before I realized my mistake and we both dissolved into nervous giggles.

'I don't think we can shake hands!' she said. 'Listen, connect with me on Instagram and if we're ever allowed to have fun again, come over for a barbecue,' she offered, before scribbling her name down on a piece of paper.

I looked down and repeated it in my head. Laura Pradelska. Without doubt, it was familiar. The minute I got home I fired up my laptop and googled her name. Of course! A quick search of her Instagram account let me know. She was a *Game of Thrones* actress who played the role of Quaithe. The irony was not lost on me. Quaithe is a mysterious prophet who *only ever* appears in full mask. I smiled. Lexi had been right – here you could bump into any celebrity just going about their business.

At first, I missed the daily commute to the office and the chats with my team. But working from home full-time again did have its advantages. All the walks out with Sigi I'd promised her now became a reality. As the warm spring sunshine emerged we picked up our regular circuit around the block during my breaks. Daffodils and primroses had started appearing under the trees along the route and Sigi leaned in and sniffed them whenever we passed. Or she'd take a bite from the ivy draped across garden walls – she is the only cat I know who loves the taste of plants – a habit picked up in Golden Gate Park. Two tugs of her leash reminded her that we didn't have all day. But occasionally when I had extra time, I'd buy a takeaway coffee and sit outside at a cafe while she patiently followed the traffic.

Immediately, I noticed how people walking towards us momentarily forgot themselves and bent down to give Sigi a stroke, pulling back at the last moment with an anxious look before giving us a wide berth. 'It's okay,' I reassured a few. I was as nervous as anyone of catching the virus. The risk factor associated with Covid-19 and the unknown damage it could do felt far more scary than catching the flu, or nursing a violent hangover. That said, others clean forgot about any social distancing rules whatsoever and dived straight in.

'Oh she's so cute! Look at her.' One woman we used to see regularly couldn't resist the urge to pet Sigi. Initially I debated whether I should stop her. How the virus was passed wasn't 100 per cent clear and there were some suggestions on Twitter in those early days that it could be passed by pets. On the other hand, I'd immersed myself in the cold, hard science. The instructions were to stay 2 metres apart but most reports advised that in the open air, the chances of catching Covid-19 were greatly reduced. Just to be safe, I let Sigi out further on the leash so passersby could stop. I understood they were only being kind. What's more, it's human nature to want to interact. And that was perhaps the strangest feature of the pandemic in those first few weeks. No one knew what the boundaries were any more. Do you say hi? Stroke a cat? Or walk by stony faced and fearful with metres separating you?

Even at home, establishing a new set of boundaries was also a learning curve. Bianca and I rarely shared an office, but now we were stuck beside each other 24/7. The slightest noise, like my keyboard tapping or a work call, became irritating. 'Seriously Travis. Do you have to use a mechanical keyboard?' Bianca reached fever pitch one day in reaction to my clunky gamer-style keyboard. My computer speakers also very quickly got relegated to the living room and connected up to the TV. Overnight, headphones became a permanent accessory for both of us. And regrettably Bianca adopted my addictive coffee habit, which she's not yet been able to shake. Yet, I also felt fortunate. At least we *had* a spare room. Other colleagues lived in shared houses, confined to working from their bedrooms or parked on kitchen tables alongside their flatmates, which must have really sucked.

To create some space between us and also to give myself a distraction, I started to make a list of jobs that I'd been meaning to do, but hadn't yet got round to. First on the list was to build a cat tree in the living room for Sigi and Ylva. I'd ordered it a while back, but it had sat in its box.

Cat trees are something I'd had at home in San Francisco, from ever since I brought Ylva home. Only a few days in to her arriving with us she'd started to become ill with a nasty diarrhoea bug. Although we confined her to the study where her litter tray sat and kept her warm and hydrated, nothing seemed to work and we watched as she became scarily thinner. Eventually, we discovered she had giardia – a tiny parasite that lives in a cat's intestine but one that causes so much distress, especially to kittens whose immune system is weaker. Now, I think it's why she still occasionally screws up and pees on our bed – she has an anxiety about using her litter tray.

Despite that, having rescued Ylva from the God-awful breeder I doubted her neurotic tendencies developed solely from that illness, so I'd also taken some advice from a Bengal expert. As well as placing several litter trays out for her, she told me that high perches would also ease Ylva's stress. Apparently, the higher a cat can climb the more content it is – a deep-rooted evolutionary memory from when cats needed vantage points to watch out for prey. How high a cat sits can also signal which cat believes it is the dominant animal. Ylva loved the tree from day one but when Sigi came along, who was 'top cat' became obvious. One day, I entered the living room to find Ylva cowering under the roof of the tree's highest level. I didn't notice Sigi until I heard her long, deep miaow. When I looked up she'd bypassed the tree completely and was metres above hugging the curtain pole staring down like a queen surveying her kingdom, watching Ylva's every move closely.

In London, the tree that I built was more of an elaborate adventure playground. From the bottom perch the cats could climb on to a cushion or into a cat hammock. Further up the scratching posts there was a covered den. Extra perches towered above and there was even a rope to swing from. Of course, I anticipated fights about who was sitting or sleeping where, but surprisingly this time around Sigi and Ylva took to it straight away and shared amicably from the start.

By the time I finished constructing it, it was clear that Covid wasn't going away in twelve weeks. If anything, it was growing into a deeper crisis. Whenever I could, I tuned into the daily briefings that were broadcast. Slide after slide showing infection rates, death rates, hospital admissions, public transport usage and global comparisons. As someone who deals with data day in, day out, I found the statistics fascinating, but it also struck me that none of it conveyed the entire human cost. I guess being so far from home, Bianca and I felt the isolation acutely. We'd only just settled in, and we couldn't see friends or entertain plans to see relatives. Alarmingly, the graphs' trajectory of deaths in the US shot way above that of the UK and every other European country, so we worried. In San Francisco the federal government had put in place one of the strictest early lockdowns – in hindsight something I believe Britain should also have done. And while our friends living in the Bay Area kept us updated through a shared WhatsApp group, we understood that like us some were panicked by catching the virus as well as feeling the loneliness of being stuck inside.

Most of all I worried about my friend Teresa. We had been in a relationship for several years before I met Bianca, but after it ended we'd remained close friends. She worked as an infection control nurse who travelled around the state to visit patients, often in their homes, so I made a point of checking in on her regularly. The pictures she posted on WhatsApp said it all: *Today's glamorous outfit,* she'd written jokingly on a day when she had to drive out to treat an immune-suppressed patient. I barely recognized her buried beneath her blue protective suit, mask, goggles, gloves and a plastic visor strapped to her head. I thought about the San Francisco humidity and how she must have been sweltering. Bianca also worried about her loved ones and spent many hours calling home. She especially missed her mother who had moved from Manhattan several years before to be near her in San Francisco. She had been excited for us when we announced we were moving to the UK but was sad to see us leave too, and Bianca and her kept in touch most days. In truth, the both of us were going slightly crazy. Work kept us occupied during the day but by 6pm the evenings already had a never-ending monotony to them. Nowhere to go. No one to see. Just us and Sigi and Ylva.

One evening it felt like a lucky break to hear our doorbell ring – a sound we hadn't heard in quite a few weeks. 'Who is it?' I shouted as I entered into the hallway. It felt weird to even ask.

'Lexi,' he shouted before I opened up. Outside Lexi was hovering in the lobby, tapping his foot impatiently. 'Hey guys, wondering whether you'd like to come up for a drink?' he asked, his voice sounding desperate. With the pubs shut and everyone indoors, he had been feeling the isolation too. A real estate agent by profession, he'd also been one of the first workers to be put on the government furlough scheme which had been announced that month. Under furlough, workers would still get paid but weren't actually allowed to work. Certainly house viewings were off-limits and it was obvious the boredom was creeping in.

I hesitated, and the worse thing was I could see that he sensed it. His head dropped and his eyes searched around the floor.

'Please come up. I'm going out of my mind!' he begged. In the months since we'd met him, Lexi was probably the most sociable person we knew. Whenever we stepped inside The Washington, he was there. I understood his frustration, and I felt ashamed to question his generous offer.

'I'm not sure we can, Lexi. Are we allowed?' I asked.

'I think so. We all share communal space anyway.' His face broke into the widest grin.

While we were technically two separate flats, he believed that we were considered to be one big household, and if we wanted to we could socialize together.

'We can check, but I don't think that's in the rules,' I said.

'Mum and I would love the company,' he replied looking

disappointed. I couldn't blame Lexi. We all wanted life to return to normal so badly.

On that occasion we all reluctantly agreed not to, but by July – the time when two households were permitted to gather indoors – we were quick to arrange an evening together, and many more nights followed. And when I think back now, I realize what a saviour those evenings with Lexi and Mary became. Mary is well into her seventies and as we sat drinking and chatting, it turned out she'd been a wild child in her youth – part of London's Swinging Sixties, modelling and also living in Greece where she'd met Lexi's father. In between leaning out of her kitchen window to have her cigarette, she entertained us over wine and beer with story after story.

6

LIFE SUPPORT

Can we talk Travis? I suggest you come in and we meet. The email from Brandon had been friendly but matter-of-fact. It was now the beginning of June and we'd been working at home for almost three months. Although we received regular updates on the health of the company, it had been a while since he and I had sat down face to face. We were due a catch-up.

For the tech team of which I was a part of, the message so far had been business as usual. Sales, on the other hand, had borne much of the workload. As start-ups go the company had been doing well and expanding its client base and employees before lockdown, but being a payroll platform its revenue was dependent on a whole bunch of businesses staying afloat. Predictably, some had scaled back immediately after lockdown was announced, and a handful had already gone bust. Replacement clients needed to be found. In fairness, Brandon and his co-founder Mark had been communicating continuously with staff through the company intranet: the certainty of anything had been thrown into doubt, they cautioned, and if the pandemic continued there was every chance that further changes would have to be made, the extent of which no one knew.

Despite the warnings, I felt upbeat as I boarded the bus. What I hadn't expected was the feeling of other-worldliness that hit me as soon as I stepped on. It was the first time I'd used public transport since lockdown started. The plastic screen now shielding the driver from passengers felt as cold and emotionless as my mask. 'Hi . . . thanks,' I said hesitantly as I tapped my phone on the sensor, but the driver stared straight ahead. The upper deck was empty. Normally, I'd be struggling to find a window seat. As the bus weaved its way through its regular route, the streets looked hollowed out of traffic and people, as if the whole city had been shaken inside out: not the London I'd moved to nine months before but an abandoned town.

When I arrived at work, Brandon was already in his office dressed in his usual jeans and untucked blue shirt. 'Hi man, good to see you again,' I said taking off my mask and half-waving an awkward apology. Brandon smiled weakly and for the first time, I sensed this wasn't just a casual meeting.

'I'm sorry, Travis. I'm going to get to the point,' he said as he poured me a coffee and sat down to face me. My chest tightened as I tried to read his expression. Worse-case scenarios began to ricochet around my head. Was my job over? If that was it, was there anything I could do to change it? What would I tell Bianca? We'd not long signed a two-year rental agreement on our apartment that had pushed us to the limit of what we could afford. Sigi and Ylva loved it there. How could we live without my salary?

I stared back at Brandon, bracing myself for the blow. He was normally such an upbeat guy – a real energizer and an inspirational leader – but I could see whatever was coming was not easy for him either.

'We've had to rethink, Travis. We've decided to put a whole bunch of people on furlough with immediate effect. You're on the list,' he continued.

Furlough? *Oh Jesus fucking Christ! Thank fuck.* 'Oh . . . okay . . . thanks, man,' I replied. I'd felt a lump rising in my throat but now I didn't know whether to burst into tears or hug Brandon. 'For how long?' I hesitated. In truth, work had been so full-on since I arrived that the idea of being paid to take a break suddenly seemed attractive. My only concern was how much of a break. The office and its daily interactions with my team, even the fun stuff that got fired back and forth on our pet Slack channel had been a lifeline for me, especially since Bianca and I were so far from home and now seriously missing friends and family.

'We're going to see how things go. But don't worry, we'll get you right back. We'll re-evaluate in August and by September we should be good to go,' he reassured me.

What made me feel a lot calmer is that I hadn't been singled out. Around a quarter of the company would be furloughed, mainly people like me from middle management, freeing up enough revenue to compensate for lost business. Brandon explained that staff could be made non-essential for a while and we'd all restart together. We'd continue to dial into the weekly all-staff meeting to keep up to date ready for our return.

'Sure man. I understand,' I said, and I really did mean it. Brandon wasn't only my boss, he was also an owner with a business to run. It wasn't personal and I knew him to be a good guy at heart. What's more, I also knew he wouldn't have taken any decision lightly. He and I went way back. He knew how at times I'd struggled in San Francisco and how, when he offered me the job, I was at a low ebb. What he had no clue about was that on the day we'd met two years previous, he'd saved me. Had he not messaged me on that day, it's likely I would have gone through with a plan to take my own life.

When I look back now, it's clear that working in Silicon Valley on and off for almost 20 years had taken its toll. But when I'd arrived fresh from Washington State aged 23, it felt like the most exhilarating experience of my life. I still remember parking up my Honda, stretching out my legs on the main road in Palo Alto and breathing in the hazy afternoon air. A few months down the line and I would have been able to spot someone who looked exactly like me that day – that same hillbilly guy who'd stepped in from out of town, who'd turned up wearing ill-fitting jeans and a flannel shirt and who hadn't yet cottoned on to how to survive. San Francisco, and especially Silicon Valley, is all about what's on show – what's conspicuous – and it didn't take long for my perspective to shift. After all, these were the years of the dot.com bubble.

For a kid who'd grown up in the depressed towns and cities of the Pacific Northwest, and who'd fought to keep himself in paid-for education, the extravagance of America's West Coast felt super-saturated in *Wizard of Oz* technicolour. Every Friday, the work fridges got flung open and the Budweisers began to flow. Afterwards we'd pile into town and get wasted on beer and tequila shots. Whereas before, I'd existed with my head down, diligently working my odd jobs for Bryan, here the separation between boss and employee didn't exist. Bleary-eyed in the early hours of any Saturday morning, it wasn't uncommon for your chief executive to be drunkenly corralling everyone into 3am conference room karaoke, or to be shoving dollar bills into the panties of exotic dancers in whatever strip bar we'd ended up in. Or you'd find yourself at a pool party in a condo in the hills where some bright spark stripped off naked and dived in, encouraging everyone else to take the plunge. Maybe because I'd been solitary for so long, I embraced all of it. Besides, in California I discovered that I could hide between the cracks in my past.

'Hey man, where did you get your Ph.D?' I remember being asked that question on many occasions when I started working in Palo Alto. Part of me ballooned with pride. This wasn't a question being asked by anybody. These were people with degrees in biotech or biology, most likely graduates from Stanford University or MIT. *Wow, I'm good enough for them to assume I even have a degree?* I thought. Yet another part of me squirmed inside. At home, I was the outlier: the guy who defied the odds and got himself the hell out of there. Here I was nothing more than an amoeba in a gargantuan pond. While I tried hard not to show it, I knew I wasn't one of them.

'Well, I studied computer science,' I mumbled embarrassed, hoping I wouldn't have to explain that it had only been a few courses at a community college. I knew that would not be the high-status currency that some colleagues often loved to trade. Water cooler conversations revolved around who was buying which million-dollar condo or which BMW they were driving. Years later that would morph into which model of Tesla. I could sense their interest deflate as soon as the words dropped from my mouth.

Yet as time went by and I had a foothold in the industry, I didn't have to explain myself. No one cared how few qualifications I had on paper because through a network of contacts I'd tapped into, I could easily move around. From the biotech firm where my monthly wage barely sustained a rental apartment, I joined NetCurrents. It was a company set up by a new-economy entrepreneur. Businesses paid us to manage their reputation through analysing chat room data – interactions about brands that were positive or negative – and helped them form strategies around products and campaigns. Overnight, I doubled my salary. A few days after my first pay cheque landed I went out and bought my very first sports motorbike. Now I was the owner of a bright yellow and black Honda CBR600 – a wasp on steroids. I sent my dad a picture, and I rode out on it wherever and whenever I could through the twists and turns of the Los Altos Hills, partly to show off. In future maybe I'd buy that BMW or that condo too.

I was two years in when I got my first taste of how cut-throat the tech industry was. In the year 2000 the dot.com bubble burst. Spectacularly. In the space of a few months, Silicon Valley atrophied into a kind of Death Valley, and while I wasn't the guy from out of town any more, I *was* naive. So far, work hadn't always felt fair or easy but I'd been treated with respect. Bosses let me know I was a liked and trusted member of any team but when the crash hit I began to understand how disposable people could be.

When I'd arrived in the late 1990s, the whole area had been dripping with tech start-ups promising to change the world. 'Get big fast' was the dominant credo. Venture capitalists swarmed in, poised to reap the rewards of supernova valuations divorced from any actual profitability. Not that I fully understood it then, but most companies were bloated on debt selling products or services at a loss to corner market share, so when they floated on the Nasdaq the early money could cash out. Get big fast became get rich quick. It worked for a while but behind the branding and the glitzy advertising the financial foundations of so many businesses were perilously shaky. One by one they began to fold.

That's exactly what happened at NetCurrents. I was fortunate enough to remain employed for a short while after the crash. As the only guy in the building who understood how to operate the company's servers, I became its last salaried employee, but the writing was on the wall. A bunch of workers got laid off immediately, and a few weeks later everyone else's pay cheques started bouncing. There were no all-staff emails keeping us updated. No meetings. Just an information vacuum and the drip, drip feel of a business going under. Then, I got a call from its founder.

'Travis. I'm flying in from LA. Meet me at the W downtown. Let's talk about how we keep this show on the road,' he said in his gravelly voice.

The W is a luxury hotel in San Francisco and when I got there Irwin was sat in the foyer bar, one hand resting on his distended stomach and the other holding a china coffee cup.

'We'll keep the servers running and operate a skeleton staff,' he proposed.

'My last pay cheque bounced,' I told him. 'If you want me to keep working, you're going to have to pay me.'

'You'll get paid, son. We'll be back in business when this blows over,' he promised, before reaching into his wallet and pulling out his own personal chequebook.

'Here, take this,' he said, signing off an amount that wasn't even half of what I was owed. The cheque didn't bounce, but it did turn out to be the last pay cheque I ever received from NetCurrents. Within weeks any remaining employees were looting the offices, taking whatever computers or furniture were left before the doors shut for good. Many of them had families to feed and they'd suffered months of lost earnings. For me, it was a sucker punch of a different variety. Landing that job proved to me and the world I was capable – everything my family thought I couldn't be. I was making a living, earning a good wage. It had been my dream since I'd sat in my attic room in Washington State teaching myself how to programme. I couldn't go back. Besides, even if I'd wanted to, I knew I would be treated with all the suspicion of an out-of-towner. On the few occasions I had visited home, there'd been the odd barbed comment. 'God, you make so much money now, Travis. Sorry if the food's not good enough,' I remember my mum saying as I ate in a local restaurant with her and David. It was the kind of passive-aggressive line my mum excelled at. Maybe it was a compliment, maybe it was a put-down – it was often hard to tell and in some ways comments like that made me proud that I'd spread my wings, even though her lack of encouragement always felt deflating.

Another thing I recall is the disappointment of discovering that nowhere served espresso – back home it was still the same diner-style coffee that there ever was, not coffee from the barista bars of downtown. And the hot dogs and fries tasted like cardboard compared to the fresh fish, Hawaiian pokes and Mexican burritos I'd gotten used to. By comparison San Francisco was an international melting pot. Nothing had moved on in the time since I'd left Washington State – only me.

The second problem was that my lack of on-paper qualifications now *did* matter. With so many companies going under, any application I submitted didn't get a second glance. The competition felt fierce and in a narrowed pool of candidates the Ivy League graduates naturally won out. Rejection after rejection deadened me, and the savings I'd been living off were also whittling down month by month. After a while I started to panic and gave up entirely. I didn't see it at the time, but it's probably the moment when my mental health showed its first proper signs of fracturing too.

For the next year or so I sofa-surfed with friends or girlfriends: not a healthy or stable arrangement but I would rather have been homeless than to have headed home. I found work in a bicycle light factory in Cannery Row in Monterey some distance down the coast. I'd been seeing a girl whose family lived there and it seemed like a convenient place to move. The assembly line was monotonous and the pay sucked, but it was easy-going and gave me a structure to my day. In my mind, it was always temporary until I got back on my feet again – unlike if I'd ever stayed in the Pacific Northwest where a dead-end job could have defined my life. I spent most evenings hanging out in bars and I made friends, two of whom I'm still in touch with today.

Just as the tech industry showed signs of picking up around 2003, I eventually managed to land a job with the US Department of Defense, a branch of which was stationed not far from where I was living. A role gathering environmental data to inform troops stationed abroad was interesting enough, but the hours weren't great. Sometimes I'd get woken at 4am to travel in and update the system. Every time a marine battalion altered its course it was my job to record their observations and provide them with localized environmental forecasting. The highly classified data got sent over and I'd update the coordinates.

What it did provide me with was a decent, steady salary – enough to decide that after a couple of years I wanted to leave the US altogether and finally fulfil my ambition of going to college and getting a degree. The crash had been a wake-up call, and as far as I was concerned not having any higher qualifications was the only obstacle holding me back. It wasn't even about acquiring extra skills. I'd amassed so much experience by myself already. Underneath I felt I lacked that breezy confidence that I'd seen in so many others, and higher education seemed the key. Using my own savings and after taking some private loans, I enrolled on a course in international business and technology management in Brussels. As it turned out, studying in Europe was far more expensive than a California state school, but I wanted the experience.

Yet it was when I returned home a graduate that my life began to properly spiral. Investing in a degree had been worth it because when I started applying again for jobs in Silicon Valley, I struck lucky. An online casino games company were in need of a back-end programmer. Like the defunct NetCurrents, it was being run from Hollywood. After only a few months of getting the job, an opportunity arose. I was the eighth employee to be hired, but back-end developers like me weren't so hard to find. On the other hand, my line manager was struggling to attract games developers. It had been a while since I'd worked on any games, but I had the experience of being a dedicated gamer, learning C++ language to run *SneezyMUD* all those years ago and, in the interim, teaching myself Flash programming used for animation graphics. I approached the chief technical officer, Deswan, with my portfolio.

'Let me make a game. Give me a shot,' I suggested.

Surprisingly, it didn't take much persuasion. One of the more impressive graphics I'd created in Flash was of a fully modelled mechanical clock, gears and all, and because many of the company's online games also used Flash programming he agreed to trial me. There was an added jackpot too. According to every employee's contract, there was a rising scale of bonuses starting at $10k. High performers who created a successful game were promised an unlimited amount proportionate to the game's performance. As it was early days, no one had received it yet and to be honest it wasn't my main motivation, either. I was capable and I wanted to prove it, but Deswan used it as a carrot to dangle in front of me – if I brought him a bestselling game, a bonus of around $150,000 would be mine. Knowing that, I worked extra hard.

It was at that company that I also met Brandon. Around that time, we didn't cross paths too much. As a developer I wasn't in his team, but I knew him to be a super-smart, switched-on guy. He headed up the data arm of the business and he had a work hard, play hard reputation. It wasn't long before he got to know who I was, though. The game that I built – an online version of the classic bingo game – took two months to design. When it launched it was popular – though no more than any other game – but over the next few months I refined it, adding new features then testing it and tweaking it: bonus balls that players could buy after the main draw had been called, giving them an extra chance to win; or building complicated patterns so players could enjoy extra winning lines. It transformed it from a mediocre seller to a runaway success. Over the course of a few months it racked up millions of dollars in revenue. Deswan called me into a meeting in the main boardroom office. I arrived knowing that the bonus was mine.

These days, I've become attuned to the uncomfortable shuffle of bad news, but at that time I could not have predicted what was about to hit me. Deswan stared at me for a few seconds, then he took a deep breath. 'I'm truly sorry Travis. This is out of my hands, but head office have decided that the bonus structure is too high a payout. They're cancelling it,' he announced.

I could barely breathe. This had to be a mistake. 'They're *what*?'

'I'm furious on your behalf. I promised it to you. But it's out of my hands,' he repeated as I stared blankly across the table.

'How can they just do that?' I asked Deswan, but deep down I knew exactly how. These weren't decent people. These were Hollywood sharks with a vast corporate legal department. They could do whatever they wanted. Sure, I could take legal action, but what would be the point? The cost of any lawsuit would have bankrupted me. Besides, how many small guys like me take on big companies like them and win?

'I'm so sorry, Travis,' Deswan apologized again, and many times afterwards. Once word got round the company, I also received a deluge of supportive messages. The gut-wrenching unfairness of it stung hard, not just for me but for every other employee too. Head office had cancelled my bonus but also removed the clause from everyone else's contract. The message was clear: you work hard for us, and we'll screw you.

Away from the office, I'd found it near impossible to carry on. It felt like a rejection of everything I'd built for myself and it slowly ate into me, like the way that rust corrodes metal. Every morning I woke with a dull fog clouding my brain. Now, I think it's probably how a whole bunch of people operate in Silicon Valley. It's a destination built on dreams but only a tiny handful of people ever get to realize them. Instead, people wake up, drive to work, sit at their desks and function like the star of their own

Truman Show, hoping hard work and honest ambition will get them rewarded. Scratch the surface and so many lives are one step away from needing life support.

While I would have loved to have handed in my notice there and then, I didn't have that financial luxury. However, not long after, I did leave the design department and moved into Brandon's data team. He'd been one of the first people to drop me an email and made no bones about how outrageously he thought I'd been treated. However much I liked working for him, though, in the end I found being there too difficult. The money the game had made grew the company's operations around me. By the time I walked around a year later it had expanded from 20 to 200 staff, even hiring superstar games designers who had been heroes of mine since I was a teenager.

Fast forward seven years and my faith in people from that time was restored a little bit, because what was reassuring to discover was that Brandon had remembered everything. Not long after I accepted the job in London he wrote me an email: *I promise to work so incredibly hard to make up for the $$$ that those guys essentially stole from you,* it read. That acknowledgement really mattered, far more than he ever knew.

For the time that I remained in San Francisco, though, I began to realize that I needed help. On some days, I could barely lift my head above the duvet and make it in to work. I considered taking time off, but decided talking to anyone about how I was feeling was off-limits. Maybe a line manager would have been sympathetic, but I doubted it. At that time mental health was never discussed at work and certainly not in male circles.

Instead, everything in Silicon Valley revolved around how many hours you crammed in, how stupid hard you worked, what crazy targets you met and whether or not you could feign 'normality' throughout all of it. When I thought about moving jobs, even the recruiters I met with encouraged me to be *that* person.

'Don't worry I'll get you a new job in no time, Travis. I can see you're that type A kind of guy,' I remember one telling me not long after I put my feelers out. I was a high performer for sure, but working a 70-hour week, making a company rich with no reward, had left me feeling powerless. In the end, I understood the alpha guy to be the guy who recruiters *wanted* me to be, not who I was. Instead, I went to see my doctor and I also put my name down for a course of talking therapy. Far from helping, both exacerbated the problem. Wellbutrin, the antidepressant I was prescribed, had the strange effect of dulling my senses further but also set my mind racing – a big dipper of depression and delirium that sent me into a continuous tailspin. On most nights it became impossible to sleep which then snowballed into struggling to stay awake at work. After a few months, I went cold turkey and threw away the pills.

Talking therapy was equally as disappointing. I guess maybe I was unlucky. Inga, the super-sweet counsellor I was assigned, was Norwegian. Once she'd learned about my Norwegian background she warmed to me, but in an overly passive way. I wanted a therapist to look at my life and tell me why I pushed myself so hard or how I could stop the internal chatter of self-criticism and inadequacy that I felt on most days.

'You're doing well. You're successful. It's good to push yourself,' she said.

'If it was fine, I wouldn't feel this way,' I replied.

But Inga spent our sessions nodding sympathetically. After a while, I stopped seeing her.

A new job in the data department of the games company SEGA put me on an even keel for a short while. I met Bianca there too, although we didn't start dating until after I'd left the company. As it turned out, I didn't have too long to wait until that end point came. The year I joined hadn't been as profitable as the company had expected and when redundancies were announced I was in the 'last in, first out' cohort. It was the same story everywhere. Staff were brought in to design games and when they became surplus to requirements they got laid off. People got shunted around like a whack-a-mole game.

Next I joined Warner Bros. the penultimate death knell, where, laughably now that I look back on it, I received an official warning in the first month for over-clicking my mouse. The noise apparently disturbed colleagues. Finally, in 2017 I joined a robotics start-up called Anki where the pressure to meet targets felt off the scale. The intensity of it brought me further to collapse, then I got laid off once again.

But it was in the run-up to being laid off that final time that I could see no end to the unbearable mental pain. Four years of instability had chipped away at all the self-esteem I'd banked through getting my degree. I'd even gone back on antidepressants, this time a cocktail of two daily medications – venlafaxine and mirtazapine – known fittingly as 'California rocket fuel'. Initially it felt blissful – like a hand pulling me up from a gluey swamp – but as the months wore on those drugs destabilized me more than the Wellbutrin ever did. If I started a day, I had no clue if I would ever finish it. It took every shred of energy to put on a convincing show in the office but as soon as my lunch hour rolled around, I slipped out and walked for an hour, maybe two, trying desperately to calm the mania that had gripped me with the rhythm of each step. *How can I stop this? How can I get out?* I kept asking. Wild scenarios flashed through my wired mind before I tried to straighten myself up, walk back through the polished marble reception, take the lift to the second floor and creep back behind my desk before anyone could notice.

By the time Bianca and I started dating, and then moved in together, I was so adept at burying how badly I was handling my life behind that charade, she had no inkling of what thoughts were rattling through my head on a minute-by-minute basis. Looking back, my persuasiveness was frightening. On better, rational days I reminded myself that I'd got out of the Pacific Northwest. I'd made a life for myself. I'd created a bestselling game. I could carry on. But mostly, I saw no way back from the onslaught of depression. Even Ylva and Sigi, who had been with me during that whole time and who I loved, couldn't snap me out of it and stopped giving me any pleasure. *Who would miss me?* I thought. Instead, I existed in a ghost-like state, unresponsive to everything positive around me.

As that summer rattled on, Bianca said she was also feeling the pressure at work and needed a change of scene. 'Hey Travis, why don't we tour around Europe for a month over vacation?' she asked me around a week before I got laid off from Anki.

'Sure,' I agreed, but secretly I'd spotted a darker opportunity. Bianca's mother could look after the cats while we travelled to France, Germany and elsewhere. Some friends from the Bay Area were also going to be in Croatia where there was a music festival so we could hang out with them. Bianca would return to the States a little early to begin work, but I planned to stay on for three extra days on my own in a random country, in a random city, destination to be confirmed. That's when I'd book myself into a hotel and overdose. None of the details were clear, but there was time to plan.

And then the weirdest thing happened. A couple of weeks before we were due to fly to Paris I posted up a picture of the Eiffel Tower on my Facebook page with a status update. Looking at it now, maybe I was subconsciously searching for a lifeline:

Funemployment starts tomorrow . . . got laid off. Next couple of weeks are dedicated to working on car-related projects and taking care of some stuff that I've been procrastinating on due to my incredibly stressful work situation. Then, a month of vacation in Europe for August then I'll be back in September and ready to job hunt all over again . . . that's tech for you! Maybe I'll get into stripping!

That evening, I logged on to find a message from Brandon: *Hey Travis. You're going to be in Paris! I'm in London now and running a start-up. Do you have time to drop by? Call me . . .*

Brandon? I wasn't expecting that. A message out of the blue from him was a real surprise. We hadn't seen each other for over a year.

Sure, I found myself writing back robotically. I'd call him when I got to Europe and maybe we could meet for a few beers if I made it to the UK.

That evening, as I lay on the sofa with Sigi on my chest I found myself daydreaming about Brandon's message. *London? That could be interesting.* I felt surprisingly buoyed by it, even though I wasn't sure why Brandon had messaged to tell me. Then, without even trying, I found myself feeling hopeful for the first time in months. Another wild idea flooded into my brain. *If I asked her, maybe Bianca would marry me?* We'd been going out for around two years. Suddenly the fog started to clear a little.

On our first night in Paris, still jet-lagged from the flight, I proposed to Bianca underneath the golden glow of the Eiffel Tower. She said yes without skipping a beat. I felt like the luckiest guy in the world. And those three days when I had prepared to be alone in a hotel room after Bianca flew home turned into three days in London listening intently as Brandon strode up and down in front of a whiteboard explaining the ins and outs of his new company. *Maybe he just wants to tell me about it all or ask for some advice?* I thought as the time ticked on.

When he eventually stopped for breath, he turned to me. 'Can you start tomorrow?'

What? Brandon wasn't even joking. I looked at him in disbelief.

'I need people I can trust, Travis. Come work for me.

I promise we'll have a ton of fun,' he said. In that moment, it felt as if the last few years and months and weeks had lifted from me. A weightlessness I hadn't felt in a very long time. I was capable, and needed.

'Sounds awesome', I laughed, 'but can I finish my vacation and fly home first?'

At the start of the next week, I logged on remotely and began my new life. Those hopeless thoughts of *Who would miss me?* and plans of suicide gradually receded into the background to a more remote, unthinkable possibility.

7

BACK IN THE SADDLE

On the morning the package arrived, Sigi waited at the top of the stairs curious at the sudden bustle of activity. If I couldn't work during furlough I needed something to fill my time. I'd ordered a new bike online, given that no shops were open. The delivery driver had already called to remind me that he was strictly forbidden to step inside the hallway. Instead, he arrived in full protective gear and waited by the open door stretching out his gloved hand and a pen with the delivery note.

'Nelson? Just sign here,' he shouted before jumping back in his van, leaving me to haul the box up two flights of stairs. Sigi reluctantly manoeuvred out of the way, all the time watching with a quiet fascination.

Furlough had gifted me two months. The UK government had announced that the support scheme would finish by the end of August, and that was when Brandon suggested that he and I regroup for a chat. No one knew what help would be available after that, if any, but surely by then I'd be back in the office and leading my team.

While the break was welcome, I did worry about it. As that first Monday rolled around I'd forced open my eyes in the half-light of the early morning and pulled back the covers. *Got to get up for work,* I thought. I was on autopilot, already feeling that start-of-the-week anticlimax. The second I fully came around, the realization hit me: I had no work. *Should I pull up the duvet and snuggle under for a few hours longer? Or get up, make some coffee and say hi to Bianca?* The internal debate raged in my head for several minutes until I sat up and gave myself a good talking-to. Bad habits are hard to break once they start. The last thing I wanted was to be catapulted back to the manic depression of two years previous. Too much time on my hands might let the demons in. Of course, I looked forward to taking Sigi out for walks and I'd done my best to keep up our daily routine while I'd been working from home, but I also realized that I needed something else to get my teeth into.

One of my passions in San Francisco had been to ride my bike. Every week or so when times were good I'd take myself off towards the Upper Great Highway running parallel to the dunes at Ocean Beach. The warm wind against my skin and the sound of sand crunching beneath my tyres made me feel alive. The vista out to the teal-blue ocean allowed my mind to wander for a while. Further on I'd hit the Presidio where a network of bike trails twist and turn through parkland and coastal bluffs, or I'd ride along the promenade to Golden Gate Bridge before looping back through Golden Gate Park towards home. If I had extra time, I'd ride further into town and return on a cycleway known as The Wiggle – a mile-long zigzagging route – that follows the old watercourse of the San Francisco valley. In all, the round trip took two or three hours depending on my route.

Back then, I owned a standard road bike but mostly I rode a fixed-gear bike, the difference being that with fixed-gear you have to pedal continuously. The endorphin hit of the uphill sprints pulsed through me as I powered up to Lincoln Park from Ocean Beach, past its presidential memorial built in honour of Abraham Lincoln, and up further still until I reached the Presidio. Conversely, the pedalling rhythm of the flats had a strange soothing feeling. When I was feeling lazy I used the road bike so I could coast along.

Had it not been for a break-in only weeks before our move, I would have shipped my road bike across to London. That day, I'd arrived home from work to find the garage door wide open. Its padlock had been smashed and the twisted metal strewn on the pathway. The weirdest part was that of the hundreds of dollars' worth of tools hanging on the walls, plus a fully restored classic car, the thieves had only been interested in a bike. A small consolation, but it irritated me nevertheless. In the run-up to leaving I hadn't had chance to replace it and there'd been no point in shipping over the fixed-gear which was virtually on its last legs and ready for the dumpster.

As I was still drawing a salary over furlough until August, it felt like an investment to splash out on another: an opportunity to get back in the saddle. I also figured that cycling could be the perfect exercise during a pandemic. By June 2020, over 40,000 people had lost their lives to the illness. The rules of lockdown had been eased, but only slightly. Until mid-May we'd been allowed out to pick up essentials or to travel to work if we needed to. Now we could exercise with a friend so long as it was outside and we observed the 2-metre rule. It felt like a sliver of hope. Plus, cycling ticked all of those boxes, the added bonus being that I could discover more of the city. I'd been getting to love London and all its nooks and crannies before lockdown. At least this way, I could salvage some pleasure.

'Hey Sigi, come have a look,' I called, as I dragged the box into the study. She was already sniffing around its corners as I picked up my pocket knife and began to slice open the gaffer tape seals. At that sound, Ylva also shook herself awake and immediately sat bolt upright in her new favourite spot: the open top of my tool trolley on top of the filing cabinet.

Admittedly the bike I'd chosen was more expensive than I could realistically afford, but as I'd set myself a goal to ride out most days, and spending on recreational activities was mostly off the cards, I wanted it to feel like a treat. I'd like to think Sigi helped me choose it too. Only days before, she'd hopped up on the desk and purred next to me following page after page of bike models flashing up on the screen, nodding her head approvingly if I lingered on a page. In the end it hadn't taken me long to decide. I headed straight to the only fixed-gear specialist in London that I knew had a good reputation: Brick Lane Bikes, which has its physical shop in the heart of Shoreditch. Thanks to the internet, its reputation had reached San Francisco, where there's been a thriving fixed-gear scene since the early 2000s, so I knew exactly where to start my search.

I also had my heart set on an Aventon frame. It's a Californian company with a pretty solid reputation. When the fixed-gear boom happened in the States lots of cheaper models flooded the market, but as far as I'm concerned you get what you pay for. This model was a Mataro – a purpose-built track bike. It wasn't top of the range by any stretch. Aventons can run into the thousands, but it cost near to £800. As soon as I lifted it out of the box, I knew it was worth every penny.

The frame looked strong and heavy, but handling it felt as light as a feather. I could have picked up its aluminium frame with two fingers. I'd chosen it in white too. It hadn't crossed my mind that Sigi might ride with me so I didn't consciously pick it to match the bright white of her coat. Instead, it conjured up a fond recollection. It was a tribute to my university days when I'd studied in Brussels. With hardly any money, I'd picked up a white second-hand 1960s Peugeot frame. When I brought it home it was already a bit battered and scratched and became more so as I rode it to death, but I loved it. Over time I converted it to a fixed-gear bike as that's what friends in Brussels rode at the time. Even then, the city was far ahead in its designated cycle lanes and bike parks, which made it easy to enjoy the city on two wheels. In most cases you could get to where you needed to be quicker than if you'd travelled by car or public transport. Sadly, when I headed back to the US I had to leave it behind, but the memory of it lingered.

Sigi and Ylva seemed to take to my new bike too, although

for a slightly different reason. The cardboard packaging it arrived in hollered 'fun time'. That was another strange feature of the pandemic: our cardboard recycling had almost tripled. Whereas before we'd walked outside and bought groceries at the supermarket, the queue on England's Lane now snaked around the corner as entry became restricted to a handful of people at a time. It took too long to wait, especially when we had both been working. From early on we were lucky enough to secure a regular slot for home delivery and to the cats' delight, everything arrived in boxes. They'd already spent almost three months in cat heaven romping around the kitchen floor while we unpacked curry pastes and pasta sauces and peppers and onions.

To cats, cardboard is like their very own soft play area, and I often think that people waste so much money buying expensive toys when a simple box can keep them entertained for hours. I read online how they love it so much because they have no ability to resolve conflict. If they sense danger their stress levels shoot up so they prefer to hide in dark places like boxes or cupboards where they feel safest. *A lot of humans feel the same way!* I remember thinking.

'Hey Sigi, want to play?' I held out the packaging that had been wrapped around the bike tyres. Immediately she swiped at it with her paw and thrust her head out to bite it, shaking her head from side to side as she tried to wrestle it from my hand. 'Want to chew?' I chucked it down on the floor in front of her while she mauled it and sunk her teeth in further.

When I turned to Ylva I sensed that she was eyeing up her next move, although as usual she was biding her time. Often Ylva won't play with Sigi purely because Sigi's muscular physique dominates her and she is forced to back off. Yet faced with cardboard Ylva's resistance is also very weak.

'Hey Ylva, you know you want to!' I teased her.

Within minutes she'd hopped down and crashed into the empty box.

'Want to play hide-and-seek?' I said, giving her a ruffle to the back of her neck. Her eyes widened and she gazed up excitedly. I closed the lid and listened as Ylva's claws ripped into the cardboard sides and she let out a deep miaow. Soon the box was turning over like tumbleweed on an open plain. With the cats occupied, I got on with fixing up my bike.

Another great thing about a fixed-gear bike is that it takes no time at all to assemble – 15 minutes tops. These bikes are pretty basic compared to a standard road bike: one gear and no derailleurs, and just a single brake up front. In California I'd got used to riding fixed-gear without brakes, where it's technically legal, but in the UK a front brake is required. That said, many fixed-gear enthusiasts do ride without one, but I never have. The police don't care as long as there isn't any trouble, but if I did end up in an accident, not having a front brake would land me in some legal hot water. And being a guest in the UK and on a temporary work visa, that could cause me some serious problems.

Half an hour later and I was ready for my first ride out, although I had no idea where. A test run should probably be close to home and at least when I looked out of the window the weather was warm and dry. I opened up Google Maps and landed on what looked like a relatively simple route. From the top of England's Lane I could turn left on to Primrose Hill Road, pedal around the perimeter of Primrose Hill to meet the top of Regent's Park before following the canal westwards and winding back towards home.

'Hey guys. See you in a while,' I shouted to Sigi and Ylva who were still nosediving in and out of the cardboard. As I carried my bike downstairs I felt a flush of excitement. It felt great to be picking up a bike again and heading out to explore.

On the roadside, I looked up as far as I could see. By now it was around 11am and typically England's Lane before the pandemic would have a steady flow of traffic moving through it. Now, other than the odd bus wheezing to a stop at the traffic lights, it was deathly quiet. Once astride I adjusted the saddle slightly and set off. Initially it felt oddly shaky, as if I was riding a bike for the first time, but within a few minutes the muscle memory had kicked in. As I reached the corner of Primrose Hill Road I became aware of my limbs pounding with each stroke. That familiar tingling sensation spread upwards through my thighs and across my body as my legs worked overtime to keep the wheels turning. I even tried a few experimental whip skids – a back wheel skid to the side – and felt a rush of playful freedom, like those early days of doing BMX tricks as a boy.

Although I knew the road well, my surroundings felt as fresh as the day Bianca and I had arrived in London. Around me the gentle swish of leaves caught my senses and I could hear birdsong. And then it struck me. There wasn't a single rev of a car engine within earshot. Further along, when I hit the towpath along the Regent's Canal I noticed the water sparkling in the sunlight and the steady chug of a houseboat passing. Several cyclists were also out enjoying the weather. 'Hey there.' I nodded as we crossed paths. People replied which also struck me as different from only a few months back. Then passers-by looked jittery, locked in their own thoughts and avoiding strangers. For the first time in four months it was as if London had breathed a collective sigh of relief as at last people could enjoy the outdoors. As I continued I also felt the stress across my shoulders melt away. I arched my back to feel my muscles pop.

When I eventually made it home, Sigi was waiting for me at the door as I clambered through with my new bike slung across my shoulder. 'Things are looking up,' I said enthusiastically as I propped it up against the wall in the study. I noticed how Sigi circled around its wheels and sniffed inquisitively at the pedals, and I gave her a pat before I headed into the bathroom to take a shower. Having powered my way up the gradual incline of Haverstock Hill, sweat was dripping from my forehead, another oddly satisfying feeling that I was reminded of.

Over the following days, I repeated the same routine: wake up, grab a coffee, open Google Maps, pick a route and head out. One problem was that London is so big. San Francisco is a tenth of its size and I knew most of its hidden corners. Here there were so many routes to choose from. At first I planned mostly short trips around home: the same circuit to Regent's Park or further eastwards to explore Camden. Each time I ventured a little further.

Online I'd also ordered a GoPro camera, a cube-shaped hand-held recording device perfect for attaching to my handlebars and filming with. I'd never used a camera on a bike before although I'd seen many other cyclists do so, mainly for safety reasons. If a driver brushes up too close or clips you on the roadside, there's a real-time visual record. With the roads emptied of snarling vehicles that wasn't an immediate concern, but I did think it would be fun to film short videos to share with Bianca when I got home. I was discovering unusual places, like the large golden dome of a mosque I'd chanced upon on the edge of Regent's Park. But I was acutely aware that Bianca still had to work. 'See you later,' I shouted if she was in the study working on her laptop.

'Yeah, sure.' Her voice sounded spiritless on some days. Successive lockdowns were getting to her, but if she could see there was a world waiting for us when the pandemic was over, then it might lighten her mood. Every evening I wanted her to feel part of my day too, so we sat together on the sofa and I replayed the short clips, pointing out whatever landmark I'd stumbled across. Besides, Bianca had never owned a bike or cycled with me, so maybe it was also my way of planting a seed.

On my trips out, I was starting to notice more. One day I headed past Regent's Park and into Marylebone, a built-up but unique part of the city filled with boutique shops. I weaved my way through its Victorian mansion flats and Georgian terraces and stopped for a breather and some water in one of the tranquil garden squares. Up ahead at one set of traffic lights I saw another cyclist. From a distance I couldn't make him out, but I recognized from the way he was pedalling that he must be riding fixed-gear. From watching more YouTube videos than I care to remember and following fixed-gear racers on Instagram I knew that many came from London's cycle-courier community, but this was the first time I'd run into one while out on the road.

I headed towards him to get a closer look. He took off fast, but from his broad-shouldered outline I became convinced that I'd seen him online too. He powered on with his helmet down and his sinewy torso plugging away, blazing across junctions and criss-crossing through streets with all the scrappy style of a renegade. To pull up close to him I needed to push down hard and sprint. When I finally got there I noticed his two-way radio mast poking out from the side of his vest and the tattoos across his lower thighs. One mapped out the design of a bike below his cut-off shorts.

'Hey, are you Rucola 63?' I shouted over and smiled.

'Yeah,' he said, turning abruptly to look me up and down.

I hadn't meant to startle him. I'd just felt a sudden impulse to say hi. Now I beamed enthusiastically to show I was a friendly face. From day one, I'd taken the decision not to wear a mask while riding as it felt stuffy and uncomfortable, and at that moment it struck me just how much human gestures really mattered.

'I thought I recognized you. I saw your Hotline video,' I continued. Hotline was a popular series of videos by a cyclist named Terry Barentsen, featuring fixed-gear riders from all over the world tearing up the streets.

In truth, I felt a bit star-struck. Rucola 63 is one of the fastest couriers. Outside of their day jobs delivering to office blocks and studios, couriers often race in locations all around the globe, from Mexico to Belgium. It's called alleycat racing – an unofficial competition where each rider ticks off a series of checkpoints in the fastest time possible, using their knowledge and skill to beat their opponents. Even before Terry hit the scene I'd followed the famous rider and film-maker Lucas Brunelle's YouTube channel, and one of the very famous races, Monstertrack – where riders career though the streets of New York – an underground fixture that has grown to cult status over the years. While Rucola 63 was never the outright winner, he was often up there on the podium taking second or third place.

'Call me Mat,' he said, nodding. I noticed while we were chatting he'd given my bike the once-over. By comparison, it looked washing-powder clean against his beaten-up frame. 'New bike?' he laughed.

'Yeah!'

Mat and I pulled over on to the roadside and continued talking. I explained how I'd come over from San Francisco and while I'd never been part of the fixed-gear scene there, I had followed it online.

'Been there several times, it's a great city,' he said before telling me about the cycle races he'd been part of in the Mission District. One, called Mission Crit, was a sanctioned race on a closed course that Mat had loved. After a while, I could see him glance at his watch.

'Sorry, don't mean to hold you up,' I said apologetically.

'No worries. I'm working at the moment. Want to ride with me for a while and help me deliver?' he asked.

'Sure, man.'

Mat couldn't have been more friendly. Along the zigzag route,

Mat and I rode in parallel whenever we could. He was constantly interrupted by the staticky sound of pick-up instructions coming through his radio, yet he was generous enough to offer me some advice in between. For right-hand turns I discovered I could run the red light. So long as I had the nerve, I could pull up in the face of oncoming traffic and manoeuvre quickly. 'If you can safely make the turn first, you'll be fine,' he advised. How I was experiencing London now was a real luxury, he explained. When the pandemic was over the streets would be crowded and cyclists needed to take calculated risks to get ahead.

After an hour or so I was mindful that I needed to head back and take Sigi out for a walk. I said my goodbyes and gave Mat my Instagram handle so that we could keep in touch. 'See you around,' he said warmly. The more I thought about it on the journey home, the more thrilled I felt about bumping into someone I'd seen randomly online. What are the chances? Besides, Mat seemed like a super-friendly guy. Probably he was around early forties so we were of a similar age, and even though our meeting had been brief I'd felt a natural bond. In the midst of a global catastrophe, his kindness restored my faith in human nature a little.

Undeniably other interactions felt like more of a mixed bag. My first longer trip outside of London was to Cambridge. Towards the end of June the days had been scorching hot and the urge to get out of the apartment, even with its windows flung wide open, was overwhelming. By now I'd also fixed up a Garmin GPS system which I attached to the handlebars, plus I'd bought a heart-rate monitor, which I strapped across my chest. I also attached speed and cadence sensors to the bike so I could follow my route and also record my rides, distances and fitness levels, which I then uploaded to an online Strava account where I could track my overall fitness. I'll be the first to admit that working in the tech industry has turned me into a data freak and I get a real kick out of following graphs, patterns and trends.

Cambridge was a trip of about 120 kilometres – a distance I hadn't cycled in some time. I wasn't up for the round trip, but I knew if I took enough fuel for my body I could get there easily and then take the train home. In California, I travelled up and down the south coast taking part in endurance challenges not unlike the Tough Mudder and Spartan Race that happen in the UK. On one occasion I'd run and jumped and sweated through desert heat and sub-zero night temperatures on the 24-hour World's Toughest Mudder challenge – one of the best experiences of my life – so I was kitted out for long haul adventures. Shipped over with our belongings was my hydration vest with room enough for 2 litres of water which I mixed with nutrition powder – a calorie and caffeine boost, the kind professional athletes use to sustain them during training. I've always sworn by the brand Tailwind and had been using it for years. Along with some energy sweets, lunch was a homemade turkey and salad sandwich.

The morning of my trip to Cambridge, as I manoeuvred my bike down the hallway, I noticed Sigi virtually blocking the door, like a sentry guard on duty. 'Excuse me, Sig.' I looked her straight in the eye, but she made no attempt to budge. Instead she stared me down. God knows what she was thinking but it had the look of: *Where the hell is this guy going now?* 'Hey Sigi, going to let me pass?' But she scowled and looked away. In the end I picked her up and placed her reluctantly on the ledge in the study to watch the cat superhighway.

The route to Cambridge twisted through London's outer limits, past the urban sprawl of Hornsey and Tottenham and along the ancient Lea Valley – once a transport corridor for industrial goods and a tangle of canals and gasworks – now, as I discovered, a fascinating green ribbon that runs up through Hertfordshire. The minute I detoured from the main road and hit the canal towpath with its overhanging foliage it struck me how I'd missed being outside with a whole day ahead of me. When the route opened out to paddocks and golden cornfields and meandering waterways it looked like a typical scene you might see in a painting by one of the old masters or in a period drama.

At times I thought how great it would be if Bianca could join me, although I reckoned as a non-cyclist it would have taken some persuasion. Being more stubborn than Sigi, Bianca needs *a lot* of persuasion. Cycling alone is one kind of experience – I've always used it as a space to clear my head, work through any problems and put life in perspective. Cycling with someone else is all about the journey and sharing the moment. I couldn't help remembering that Bianca was stuck indoors.

Further east, I had my head down when the roar of a jet engine above startled me. When I looked at the satnav I realized I'd hit the outer edge of Stansted Airport. Winding its way around the perimeter fence, I stopped for a while to watch the odd carrier plane taxi up the runway and take flight into the clear blue sky. Given that most planes had been grounded at the start of the pandemic, dozens were lined up along the terminal building like eerily abandoned metal behemoths. I tried to imagine how many would have been taking off and landing on any other normal day.

Elsewhere, thatched cottages lined the roadsides of quaint medieval villages. On occasions I had to remind myself to slow down to take it all in. Sometimes when your legs are grinding away you forget to look up, and I was loving the sheer physical effort of the ride. I refuelled on-the-go but made a mental note to take breaks. Around midday I reached a village that appeared to be more of a pass-through place: not particularly scenic but as I turned at the junction I'd spotted some picnic benches outside a local pub. *Time for some lunch,* I thought. As everything looked closed I doubted anyone would mind me sitting there. I parked up my bike.

As the sun beat down I stretched out my legs and unwrapped my sandwich. When I looked over I wondered if the pub had been forced to close. There had been so many reports of pub and restaurant owners going out of business, yet when I peered in closer I could see the faint outline of someone moving around inside. I'd made good time that morning and if it did open maybe I could reward myself with a beer and relax for longer.

Around 15 minutes later I heard the chain rattle and the red door heave open. A stout, middle-aged woman appeared with a cleaning cloth in her hand. I smiled, but she didn't look up. She didn't look much in the mood for pleasantries, so I carried on eating. 'I'm opening up now, so you'll have to move,' she growled angrily before turning back inside.

I was dumbfounded. Her cleaning cloth shooed me away like I was a fly. 'I was . . .' I launched into a reply, but I stopped myself. I was about to say I would have ordered a drink if she was serving, but I thought better of it. Maybe a man on his own dressed head to toe in Lycra wasn't the kind of clientele that was attractive in these parts of England? Not everyone loves a cyclist. Anyhow, I was nicely exhausted from the ride and I didn't want to waste my energy getting into a confrontation. 'Sorry, no problem,' I mumbled, then I packed up and continued on, mindful of the 40 kilometres ahead.

8

SIGRID RIDES

Sigi standing next to the door as I was about to leave for my daily cycle was getting to be a habit. I couldn't work it out at all. Ever since my bike had arrived she'd been curious about it, but this was verging on wilful obstruction. We were still walking circuits of the neighbourhood together so it wasn't the outdoors she craved. She wasn't being deprived of attention in other ways, either. Since I'd been on furlough I'd begun making her a chain-mail harness, inspired by my love of *Game of Thrones*. Every day, I sat down for an hour and worked strips of aluminium metal wire around an old pushrod salvaged from the engine of my Chevy Nova. Using a pattern created from one of Sigi's material harnesses I slowly built it up to create the shape, linking each chain together to form the mesh. The repetition felt so relaxing that I often lost track of time, winding each strip carefully around the rod until it formed the perfect link.

'Here Sigi, come and try.' Every so often she padded over for a fitting, giving the harness a sniff and letting me rest it across her back. It weighed no more than the usual harnesses she'd got so used to wearing. She didn't flinch once. Instead, she rested patiently while I measured round her chest and scribbled down the numbers. I felt like a tailor to the stars. To the outside world it might look a bit crazy, but I loved her new harness, in particular how the silver metallic chains glistened against Sigi's white coat.

'What do you think Sig?' I asked, propping up a full-length mirror for her to see. Supposedly cats can't recognize their own reflection but she stared back contentedly. When the harness was finally complete, I attached a lead to one of the links and placed it around her for a final fitting, this time taking a picture. I wasn't a regular documenter of Sigi or Ylva, although I did take the odd snap if they were doing something funny or unusual. Yet Sigi's majestic expression made me smile. If there was ever a feline equivalent of Daenerys Stormborn – the character played by Emilia Clarke in *Game of Thrones* with her epic icy-white hair – then Sigi was it.

'I am Daenerys Stormborn of House Targaryen, Mother of Dragons, Khaleesi to Drogo's riders and Queen of the Seven Kingdoms of Westeros,' I boomed in a theatrical voice.

Cooly Sigi raised her brow as if to say: *Guys. Meet my dad. The joker, huh?*

Sigi's behaviour had been playing on my mind, though, and in mid-August I had an idea. I'm not sure why I hadn't thought of it before. Sigi was circling around in her usual way as I collected my bike gear before stubbornly taking position by the door making it difficult for me to pass. All this time I'd thought she didn't want me to leave, but maybe she was asking if she could come too? I'd only ever taken Sigi out once before on a moving vehicle – an electric scooter that I owned in San Francisco. That time, I'd strapped her in my chest harness and ridden out to Ocean Beach to laze around on the sand dunes and listen to the waves. She'd never experienced the ocean before and while I was unsure if the expanse of water might overwhelm her, she was mesmerized, leaning into the air and following the tideline as wave after wave rhythmically lapped. She seemed to be in her element. The inner city wouldn't be so serene, but maybe it was worth a try.

The chest harness was somewhere in a box and when I fished it out, I clipped it around my body before sliding her in. Instead of resisting, she nuzzled her face against the edge of the material and I could feel the vibration of her purr as I picked her up and rested her back against my chest.

'Want an adventure, Sig?' Sigi looked up eagerly as I wheeled my bike out from the study. As the roads were quiet we could have ridden further, but for a first try I settled on the initial circuit I'd cycled around Primrose Hill and along the top of Regent's Park. I also packed Sigi's leash so we could hang out for a while. If I filmed it, I could show Bianca later, but now the dilemma was how to capture Sigi in the frame. Any videos that I'd made before were of a simple forward view. This time I secured gaffer tape around the handlebars and positioned the lens as best I could to point directly at Sigi.

'Ready for your first movie?' I joked.

On England's Lane Sigi seemed super-engaged, looking up, down and all around, but it struck me how setting off felt different for me. So far I'd spent six weeks cycling on my own not worrying about my safety. Now Sigi was on board I was going to have to be extra-cautious. Dodging red lights was out of the question. That said, in all my years of cycling I had only ever had one serious accident. At the time I was studying in Brussels and happily drifting down a segregated cycle path and through a green light. The last thing I remember is a car turning in front. *Bang!* Everything after that came to a stop. It had been the day after a World Cup final, and when I came to I was lying in a pool of my own blood in a pile of empty beer bottles at the side of the road. A searing pain hit me. The impact had jolted my pelvis so hard against the handlebar stem that the bone had snapped like a twig. I lay there, half conscious, listening to a siren approaching before I was eventually lifted into an ambulance. I needed stitches in my arms and legs where the glass had cut me. At the hospital I was also unable to walk without crutches but when doctors first allowed me to stand they gave me only one to rest on. As I hauled myself up, a stabbing pain shot through my leg like a spear being driven into it and I passed out instantly on the concrete floor. It took months of recovery before I could cycle again.

Ever since then I'd been extra-cautious of turning vehicles, even in situations where I had right of way, but carrying Sigi definitely added another dimension. As we headed down Primrose Hill Road I obsessively checked to see whether she was okay. Immediately, I erupted into laughter. I couldn't see Sigi's face, but I could feel her back wriggling against my vest. Her hind legs were stretched out air-walking in a weird kind of slow motion, and her forelegs were flailing around like an upturned beetle.

'Hey, how you doing down there?' I called out. A vision

flashed up in my mind of astronaut Neil Armstrong taking his first steps on the moon back in 1969: *One small step for Sigi, one giant leap for catkind.* I listened closely, half-expecting her to let out an elongated miaow – a sure sign this wasn't working. It did look awkward. She didn't, but when we finally took a break on Primrose Hill she seemed relieved to be lifted out of the harness and leaped around on the grassy bank.

'Your first bike ride, Sigi. What did you think?' I asked, but she'd already trotted off distracted by the squirrels. After a while we headed home.

That afternoon I uploaded the short video I'd made on to a free editing program I'd found online called OpenShot. It was pretty basic software and easy enough to navigate. When I enlarged the screen I could see the camera angle had captured the top half of Sigi and my upper body, but the footage did look shaky and amateur. As I played it back I became captivated at how Sigi had taken it all in her stride. Her big blue eyes were wide open for the whole journey and her head swayed from side to side following cars and pedestrians. I also noticed how her ears were standing straight up and positioned slightly forward. Worried that may be a sign she was fearful, I did a Google search to double-check. Even though deaf cats can't hear, they still use their ears to communicate emotion and according to several specialist websites this meant she was alert and interested rather than angry or frightened. *Typical Sigi,* I thought. I found myself watching and rewatching the video, spellbound by her every move.

I made a promise to take Sigi out again, but I did need to

find a better method than the harness. As well as appearing uncomfortable, when I'd lifted Sigi out at the park she felt hot and clammy. A damp patch had also seeped through on to my chest. It couldn't have been that pleasant for her.

With only a couple of weeks left of furlough, I rushed to complete my to-do list. This included finishing off customizing my bike. When I'd first assembled the frame it was stiff and sturdy, but from the outset I'd had the urge to upgrade everything else, like I'd done with all of the previous bikes I'd owned. The saddle was so-so and if I was going to be travelling longer distances, like the journey to Cambridge, I wanted one that was just right. There's nothing worse than hobbling around with a bruised butt after a long day on the road. I also replaced the crankset which connects the pedal to the gear. This ended up being a far greater expense. If I wanted a high-end model that was durable it would set me back as much as £500. Plus I replaced the handlebars and the stem.

As I was doing the work myself, I saved on labour costs. Even so, I spent far more than I should have. New wheels alone cost close to £1,000 – a steeper cost than I'd paid for the original frame. Of course, I could have opted for cheaper brands but ask any bike nerd – once you start tinkering, it's very hard to stop and so easy to press that buy button. Was there a voice in my head telling me we were living through a pandemic and I should rein my spending in? For sure. But an even louder voice convinced me it would be worth it. When the office reopened I'd planned to ride in most days instead of taking the bus. I'd caught the bug for

cycling again and as someone who's environmentally conscious too, I saw it as an easy way to be proactive. I'd seen in cities like Brussels how a critical mass of riders can shift the ratio of cars on the road, and friends who'd been in London for longer than me commented on how the same phenomena had gradually been transforming London into a far greener city simply because more cyclists were out and about.

By now I was also looking forward to getting back to my day job. Most of my team, like Ryan and Oskar, had remained working and outside of the weekly all-staff meetings we kept in touch occasionally over WhatsApp. The break had been nice, I reported, but returning to some kind of normality would also be welcome – not that normality looked likely any time soon. Over the summer the Covid-19 infection rate had dropped and less deaths were being recorded than at the virus peak a few months before, but now there were murmurs of a second wave in the latter half of the year as the flu season kicked in. Everything still felt so precarious.

Thankfully, both The Washington and the Sir Richard Steele had reopened and Bianca and I found ourselves in one or the other at least once a week. It was no surprise to find Lexi in The Washington too. On the times we'd gone upstairs to have a drink with him and Mary, he'd appeared close to exploding with frustration if he wasn't allowed to meet friends soon. 'It's doing my nut in!' he'd told me on several occasions.

We'd also been itching to resume our social life, but in truth neither place felt the same. In the Steele, Stephen directed us to the outdoor area where customers were sitting. It was perfect for summer evenings but he was unsure as the weather got colder whether customers would enjoy being huddled together unless they were stepping outside for a smoke. At the Washington, which was more of a gastropub, we now had to book a table even if we just wanted a drink and download the menu on our phones to order remotely if we planned to eat. Under the circumstances we understood, but that spontaneous feeling of an impromptu evening felt a bit flat. Also, thank God, neither of us had caught Covid yet and I was still anxious about spending too much time in an enclosed area surrounded by strangers.

Just as he had promised, Brandon dropped me a line towards the end of August to arrange our chat. He didn't want me to meet him at the office this time, but asked if we could catch up over Google Meet that week. *Sure, man,* I replied.

The meeting turned out to be in the afternoon. I logged on five minutes beforehand and had my notepad ready to jot down the list of priorities I would need to work through when I started back. According to the all-staff updates, some replacement contracts had been found. The sector wasn't booming, but there may be enough to get us through.

'Hey Travis, how are you? Thanks for the meet,' Brandon said as his slightly pixelated image flickered up on to the screen.

'I'm good, man. How you doing? Good to see you again. We're good to go?' I said enthusiastically.

Straight away I clocked a long silence. Maybe Brandon couldn't hear me? I checked to see that I wasn't on mute. I wasn't. 'Connection okay?' I checked again. He nodded slowly before he spoke. 'I'm so sorry Travis . . .'

When I looked at the screen I could see Brandon gazing around his office, trying to avoid eye contact. 'Oh . . .' I replied, surprised. I didn't know what was coming, but his tone was not what I had been expecting. I felt a churn in the pit of my stomach. Then I watched as Brandon straightened his back and composed himself.

'The last two months haven't gone as planned. We've had to re-evaluate. We're going to have to make lay-offs. I'm so sorry Travis,' he said.

'Right, I see . . .'

From that moment on I could see Brandon talking but the drone of his voice dissolved into a monotonous white noise. I tuned in and out while my head started spinning. *Was this really happening to me again? Seriously? How many times can one person go through this?*

Brandon was still talking. 'I know I brought you all the way over here, and I'm so sorry,' he apologized.

One consolation was that I would get a month's severance pay and keep some stock options that I'd been given when I first joined the company, although I couldn't cash them in for some time yet.

'I know this is hard, Travis. Seriously man, this is really hard for us but we're trying to help folks out as much as we can,' he explained.

Money helps, I thought, but this wasn't all about the money.

'Sure,' I replied, but I could feel my body tense. My visa was specifically attached to the job. In part, it's why Brandon and I had worked on my job title being so precise – to ensure that my entry to the UK could be rubber-stamped quickly. Brandon had personally sponsored my visa, which is a requirement for any US citizen relocating to the UK. Finding another job in a company who could offer the same might not be as easy. And there was Bianca to consider too. She was only legally here as my spouse and on my visa. We'd planned for her to apply for a visa with a similar sponsorship but she hadn't yet got round to it.

'Maybe drop me a line in six months.' I could hear Brandon winding up the conversation. He was trying to soothe the blow, but I also sensed these were empty words. I was desperate for the call to end. When it did Brandon half-grimaced. I must have looked numb. 'Good luck, man,' he said before logging off.

For the rest of that afternoon I sat motionless on the couch. Other than the seemingly temporary blip of the pandemic and furlough, my life had felt relatively steady. We'd been here for a year and so much positive stuff had happened. Leaving everything behind would be a wrench. My rational mind told me that Brandon had to do what he had to do to keep the business afloat in an unprecedented crisis, but that feeling of rejection and failure began to paralyse me. Over the past two years I'd almost forgotten what that kind of rejection had felt like. This wasn't personal but it sure as hell felt like it.

For most of that week I remained on the couch playing video games. Best of all, I strapped on my virtual-reality headset and immersed myself in games like *Pistol Whip* – obliterating gun-toting enemies one by one to a banging techno soundtrack. Or *Beat Saber* where I used my light saber to slash through rooms to a heart-pumping rhythm. Mindless, repetitive, loud, fun – anything to lose myself in and try to feel some kind of lifelike pulse through my body.

In the evenings Bianca and I talked the situation over, but I felt lost for a solution. She would still be earning so we could just about keep the apartment going. I had my severance pay and a little saved so that would help towards household bills. But the uncertainty of whether we could remain in the UK rattled us. All the defences I'd built up against the manic depression I'd experienced in San Francisco felt like they were being knocked down. Life was in free-fall again and it terrified me.

Aside from my own struggles, depression runs in my family and I've never known whether I suffer from it because of an underlying chemical imbalance in my brain or because I've been exposed to it. Maybe it's both. Now I'm convinced my mother was often depressed, as did others in her family. My cousin Curtis died by suicide just after I'd moved to Belgium. It's still so vivid in my head. He and I were close when we were younger but had grown apart as we moved around and he relocated to Los Angeles. Yet I always heard about him through my family. As adults we had similar hobbies and maybe our temperaments were more alike than I realized. The circumstances surrounding his death were as bizarre as they were shocking. Just at the moment he'd loaded a single bullet into his gun chamber and positioned it against his head ready to pull the trigger his dog had jumped up on to his lap and it misfired against the wall. Unfortunately a neighbour heard the bang, then the dog yelping and she called the police. That evening, after he'd been taken into custody and charged with discharging a firearm, Curtis hanged himself in his cell. There must have come a point when he resigned himself to his fate. When my mother broke the news to me, I remember being shaken up but not speechless. Somehow I knew it hadn't come out of the blue. Another cousin on my mother's side was also rumoured to have taken his own life, this time through an overdose. No one could be sure whether his death was accidental or not.

This time around, I didn't feel suicidal but being laid off again did trigger a whole range of emotions that shifted and intensified as the days wore on. Mostly it felt like my body was eroding cell by cell. During more lucid moments I made an effort to get up and research online what to do during the pandemic if we didn't have a valid visa. Apparently, if I'd found work I'd have to leave the country anyway and re-enter under a new sponsor. I even emailed Brandon's company lawyer, desperate for some clarity. The answer came back as clear as mud:

> *Without a valid visa technically you have 60 days to leave the country after the Home Office notifies you, but everything is suspended at the moment. It's likely the Home Office will not be sending out notices, but do check back as this will restart.*

In many ways, this made our situation worse. Our only real option was to wait it out. Every morning Bianca got up to work, but I sat on the sofa holding my breath for the sound of the letter box clattering downstairs. Sooner or later that notice was going to drop, the only question was when. It made me think of refugees who arrive in the country and spend months or years stuck in an agonizing limbo unable to move forward with their lives.

On one day an official-looking letter did arrive. My heart plummeted and when I turned it over and tore open the envelope I could feel my hands trembling. The heading said Camden Council and I panicked. Being unfamiliar with the British system, I didn't know whether any Home Office notification might come through it, but when I scanned the page it was simply a summary of that year's council tax bill. *Thank fuck,* I exhaled. I could feel my tension soften as I stumbled back to the living room.

In the weeks following Brandon's call, each day dragged into the next with no end. I tried to remind myself that I'd felt like this before and something amazing had happened: *Brandon offered you a job out of nowhere and saved your life. Bianca married you. Come on Travis, hang in there.* But each day also felt like a colossal struggle. The one thing that depression robs you of is energy. I also noticed that I was drinking heavily and counting down the hours to the evenings when I could open whatever beer or wine or vodka was in the kitchen, and Bianca could join me. When I woke each morning the dull thud across my forehead gave me licence to stay in bed that bit longer. The feeling scared me.

Whereas before it had taken me months to come round to the idea of asking for help, now I felt desperate for it. I made an appointment with the doctor who put me back on antidepressants – this time a drug called sertraline. The effect would be gradual but it would calm me, he reassured. Still haunting me were the side effects of the cocktail I'd been prescribed in California. When I raised concerns, the doctor said he hadn't heard of those drugs and I wasn't to worry. 'Give this a go Travis, and come back if there's no improvement,' he said.

I comforted myself with the thought that I had to do something, but this did feel like a backwards step. I hadn't touched antidepressants in two years. *Failed again, Travis. Such a loser.* That thought circled constantly in my head, even though after a few weeks I could feel my mood slowly lifting.

As October rolled into November different stresses seemed to take over. I became anxious about my savings ticking down. And I deeply regretted spending all that money on customizing my bike. In fact, I felt like a total dumb-ass. *What the hell were you thinking, Travis?* I punished myself. If we did have to move we'd need to arrange for our belongings to be shipped back to San Francisco this time without a relocation fee. It could cost a small fortune. Several sleepless nights prompted me to scroll through my emails. Recruiters always sent job mail-outs especially from the larger tech firms who have a higher turnover of staff. Wherever I was at in my head, I probably wasn't ready to launch myself into another tech role, but needs must.

Among the approaches several jumped out as possibilities and I did end up submitting a couple of applications. One job was at the London headquarters of Facebook in an equivalent role in data management, while the other was at Google. Both contacted me within days to say that I'd been offered a first-round interview. It lifted me, but the feeling was fleeting. Reading through each job specification made me bone-tired. Plus, the interviews would last between three and five hours and include panel questions and elaborate problem-solving exercises. I rolled my eyes. *How the hell would I get through it? How would I feign being that go-getting guy for that long?* I thought. As it turned out, I couldn't have been all that convincing. Both employers notified me soon after each interview that they didn't want to take my application forward to a second round, but thanked me for my time and interest.

By December Sigi and Ylva had also faded from my focus. My despondency over our situation hadn't left much enthusiasm to spend quality time with them. I didn't walk Sigi at all. Instead I felt myself going though the motions of feeding and playing with them, but I was grateful to have them around. One of the toys I'd brought over from San Francisco was a large hamster wheel. Both cats love it even though they use it in very different ways. Watching Ylva walk on it as it spins around is like watching a fitness freak working out on a treadmill. I occasionally lost myself watching her as she pounded off the day's stress.

Meanwhile Sigi loves to be chased. Usually this starts with her seeking me out in the apartment and crouching down like she is poised to pounce on prey. The minute I stamp my foot she turns and leaps through every room as I run behind her. One night when she scampered through the living room, she threw herself on to the wheel and rushed around it furiously until she was dizzy with excitement. Then all of a sudden she forgot all about it and wandered off elsewhere. Since we'd been in the UK I'd also bought Sigi a feather toy, which she loved. I brought it out.

'Here dummy, come and get it.' I wedged its handle in the seat of the sofa and filmed her as she leaped on to it. Immediately she grabbed her paws around the feather and wrestled, punching it left then right before karate-kicking it to the floor and sitting on it until it pinged back and hit her on the nose. She repeated the sequence over and over.

'Hey, who are you? Bruce Lee?' I joked as she flipped over and her hind legs kicked out to whack it down. She was lost in the sheer pleasure of the moment. Later when she calmed down and clambered on to me, she rubbed her face against my chin and licked it before draping herself across my chest.

When I think about it now it was probably the first time I realized that the cats had become like children to me, far more since arriving in the UK. I'd never seen myself as a guy who wanted the responsibility of kids but unlike in California I understood how the cats depended on me. And just as importantly, how I had come to depend on them. *Sigi doesn't judge me, or know me as anyone else but a person who loves her and who she can have fun with,* I thought. I don't have to prove anything to her, only that I'm here. In that respect she's a very forgiving companion even though I knew I'd stopped caring for her in the way that I should have been.

'I'm sorry, Sig,' I whispered to her, as her eyelids closed and she drifted off. I rubbed her back slowly and gave her a kiss. That night I made a promise to myself to start taking Sigi out again, whatever the circumstances.

9

SIGRID RIDES AGAIN

'Travis, you need to get out,' Bianca kept reminding me. I'd shared with her my plan to step up my cycling and take Sigi with me. She was right to hold me to my word, but it wasn't always the advice I wanted to hear. I'd been out as many times as I could manage on my own since September, but the adrenaline rush of exercise hadn't done much to shake the dread of waiting for the hammer to drop. Doubtless my presence at home was starting to grate on her. Bianca had applied for a full work visa to overcome our residency problem, but the bureaucratic wheels had ground to a halt and her company was also dragging its heels over her sponsorship.

'Can you chase it? Please?' I kept pressuring her.

'I'm doing it, Travis,' she snapped back.

Without my own security I felt an urgency to know one way or the other.

In the second week in December I finally made good on my promise to Sigi. What forced me out that day, I'm not sure.

Certainly Sigi, probably Bianca hassling, but I think there was
another reason too. As Bianca and I looked ahead to Christmas
it was obvious that we would be stuck in the UK for another
year. Disappointingly Bianca's mother couldn't travel from
San Francisco to be with us, nor could we fly there. If we did,
it's unlikely we would have been allowed back into the country.
Whether we liked it or not, we were illegal immigrants. The label
felt as weird as we did.

Making the best of our situation must have been on Bianca's
mind too. 'I'm going to buy a bike,' she announced one evening.

'Really?'

'Yup.' She nodded and smiled. 'Bet you didn't see that
coming!'

She was right. Other than looking through my videos, Bianca
had shown zero interest in actual cycling, and never on a fixed-
gear bike which she always said looked far too dangerous.

'Nothing pricey,' she added.

Just as well, I thought. The reality was we couldn't afford
anything pricey. I was still kicking myself about the money
I'd poured into my own bike. She remained adamant that she
wouldn't ride fixed-gear, but she'd be happy with a second-hand
road bike off a seller's website like Gumtree.

'Can you help me choose, Travis?' she asked.

'Sure,' I agreed. It would give me a task to focus on. I wondered,
too, whether she might have an ulterior motive. If I had company
on the road maybe it would help get me out of the deep funk I
was in. My videos had lifted her spirits only a few months back.
Maybe she wanted to do the same?

That said, time was crawling for everyone. By now I could barely read the news. Deaths from Covid-19 had doubled to over 70,000. Although it hadn't yet been confirmed, another lockdown was looming. It was touch-and-go whether Christmas would happen for anyone. Like us, friends we were in contact with over WhatsApp were also grasping at anything just to feel alive. Exercise felt like one of the healthier options available to me and it would be fun to have Bianca's company. For now, though, it would just be me and Sigi.

Nevertheless, heading out that particular morning didn't seem like the smartest of ideas. A menacing band of grey cloud had been threatening rain since I'd first looked out of the window. It would only be a matter of time before the droplets hit the windowpane. When I went to look for Sigi she was curled up in the tool trolley in the study, not yet awake. Since our last trip in August, I'd completely forgotten about finding a solution to the harness problem, but on a short ride in winter at least she wouldn't overheat.

'Hey Sig, fancy coming out?' I called over as I watched her stirring. At almost that precise moment she shook her head from side to side, extended her front paws and arched her back up in a long stretch before hopping down and sashaying out to the hallway. Oddly, it felt like she instinctively knew what I was offering. As Sigi reached the door and turned, her blue eyes stared up at me. Maybe I imagined it, but I think she shot me a look that said: *What took you so long buddy?* As soon as I plucked the harness out and showed it to her, she rubbed her cheek against my shin bone. *Big applause for Travis. He's finally got the hint.*

'Not such a dummy, huh Sig?' I joked. 'Let's give this another try.'

As soon as Sigi was strapped in and we stepped outside I felt her deep purr again. Even with the sound of the wind buffeting around us, it had all the intensity of a locomotive train. It was still overcast and bitterly cold, but it looked like we may dodge the drizzle. Safe enough to strap up my GoPro to the handlebars and record the ride. Even so, I didn't want to chance being out for too long. A short route around Belsize Park would be perfect, this time taking in a few more of the surrounding streets. London is home to such a variety of architecture that you find hidden gems everywhere. Since I'd started cycling, the creamy-white Portland stone terraces that line the roads around our area stood out. The frontages appear so grand. With Sigi on board I hoped that she might be impressed too.

'Good girl, Sig,' I reassured her as we slipped into the traffic. She seemed completely unfazed. In case she got restless, I'd stuffed some cat treats into my jeans pocket. These days Sigi loves to chew on long thin strips of chicken, but back then the only treats she liked were Dreamies, though Sigi is not the greatest eater at the best of times. She tends to pick at little morsels of food – completely the opposite to Ylva who is closer to a feline trashbin and who I'm sure guzzles food as a stress reliever. When we first brought her home she was little more than skin and bones and in the first few months of having her in San Francisco we'd found her with her head buried in the food recycling caddy, pulling out scraps of meat and vegetables. After that we never left it out where she could get at it again.

Sigi didn't seem stressed at all but the slow-motion air-walking had not abated. Now she looked as if she was the star of an underwater film sequence, arms and legs outstretched, hurtling down to the depths of the ocean, waiting to be scooped up by the movie's hero and brought back spluttering to the surface. Although it calmed as we cycled further, it impressed on me that I must find a better way to carry her. A short break in the park on the way home seemed like a long shot, so I abandoned the idea and kept going, figuring that the vibration of the tyres against the tarmac would have a soothing effect. Besides, I wanted to take in more. The cream stone looked almost luminescent against the stormy sky. As I slowed down to admire it, I couldn't help thinking about London's bygone age. Most of these houses had now been converted into apartments but once they would have been country homes for the city's wealthy gentry. What about all the people who would have lived here before the Industrial Revolution? Before the world wars? Before our wild technological age? Goods delivered at the touch of a button. Global connections made every nanosecond. Money wired across borders. *That would blow minds,* I thought.

'Hey! Hey!' At that moment my thoughts were interrupted by a cry. At first I ignored it, not registering it was for me.

'Hey!' The voice from behind got louder and closer.

As I turned I caught a glimpse of a woman on a bicycle chasing me down. As she rode up next to us I could see her face beaming.

'Hey. Wow! That's so amazing! Your cat!' she called out. She didn't stop but whizzed past almost clattering off her bike as she rubbernecked to smile at Sigi. She was still giggling as she turned the corner. 'Amazing!' she repeated. 'So beautiful!'

'Oh . . . thanks,' I called ahead, a bit embarrassed. I'd gotten used to admirers if I took Sigi out for a walk. Most people who stopped wanted to know what breed she was, or what her name was, or to tell me how cute she was. But being pursued down a North London street by a cyclist? There was something bizarre but also kind of exciting about it.

'You've got a new fan,' I whispered to Sigi.

By the time I got home I was still thinking about the woman. I uploaded my footage to OpenShot and replayed it a couple of times before editing it down into a bite-sized, six-second clip. The footage was still as amateur and shaky, but the woman's expression was priceless. The camera had caught it all. Such a simple thing had made her so happy. Watching it back also gave me a brainwave. She had a wicker basket perched on the front of her bike. Not exactly unusual. So many people in London have them filled with groceries or work bags. *Would it be stretching things to put a cat in one?* I debated.

Nah, don't be a dummy, Travis. That's never going to work. Or could it? If I made the basket comfortable, Sigi could move around in a way she couldn't strapped into the harness. *Let's give it a try,* I thought. That evening I searched online for a cheap basket to trial. If Sigi hated it, I wouldn't have wasted much. If it worked, she could come out for longer.

That evening, I also posted the clip of the woman on my Instagram page. In the past, I'd rarely uploaded anything even though I'd had an Instagram account for years. In truth, I'd always been more of a voyeuristic scroller, far happier to view other people's posts. Whether it was fixed-gear races or cycling enthusiasts who I followed, I could lose hours searching and clicking and viewing. Yet I'd felt a bit self-conscious about my own stuff. The work Slack pet channel had been open to a select group of people, most of whom I knew. It had felt different. And if I ever posted on Facebook it was about keeping friends updated about our lives or sharing pictures, especially since we'd moved to the UK.

Ah, what the hell! She's my cat, I thought. There was something about being out with Sigi that I felt the urge to share.

A week later I was ready to trial the basket. The fabric did feel cheap and nasty but it slotted on to the handlebars easily enough. I wanted to see how Sigi took to it before I exposed her to the open road. If she became restless, it could become a problem. Nightmare scenarios bounced around my mind of her clambering off the sides if she got startled, or chasing after a bird and catapulting herself into the oncoming traffic. Would anyone swerve or stop? Drivers wouldn't be so sympathetic, I figured.

'Hey, what do you think of that?' I asked as I eased her in gently. Sigi pressed her nose around the canvas shell. It smelled new and plasticky. Then she circled around kneading her paws up and down to get a feel for it.

'Does it get the Sigi seal of approval?' There was only one way to find out. The safety aspect of the basket was bothering me, though. I needed to find a way to secure Sigi without constricting her. After all, the whole point was so she could enjoy the ride.

First, I put her harness on and measured the lead length. I'd have to shorten it, but if I replaced it with a bungee cord that threaded through the basket's aluminium frame then it should do the trick. Once it was attached I pulled it hard to its full extent. So long as the fixture could take Sigi's weight, the elasticated cord would give her the flexibility to move back and forth or left and right without the neck tie strangling her if she lunged forwards. 'There we go,' I said, admiring my handiwork.

Meanwhile Bianca's bike had also turned up. We'd managed to find a custom-made Glider Boxer model at a fraction of its usual price from a second-hand dealer. It had been delivered the day before. It wasn't anything fancy but decent enough for short sightseeing trips. Outside it was clear and frosty. I hadn't seen much of Regent's Park over the past few weeks and I reckoned my familiar route would be best while Sigi got used to her new chariot and Bianca adjusted to hers.

It's fair to say that once we got out, I realized I may have taken on more than I could chew.

'Okay Travis, you're going to have to cycle near to me,' Bianca demanded.

Bianca really wanted to ride with us, I could tell, but her lack of confidence kept my senses alert the whole time. To say she was a novice would be an understatement. As soon as we hit the road I felt like an overzealous parent keeping watch over two delinquent children.

'Shit Travis, what the hell gear should I be in?' Bianca shouted from behind. Bianca's bike was an 18 speed, with chain rings on the front and 9 gears at the rear. She needed a crash course.

After a quick stop on the perimeter of Primrose Hill to talk her through how gears actually worked, we set off again.

The GoPro camera was strapped to the same spot on my handlebars ready to capture Sigi's reaction. 'Okay Sigi? How's it going down there?' I shouted as we reached the bottom of Primrose Hill Road. At first Sigi crouched down in the basket as gusts of wind whipped across her head. But as the wind calmed, I noticed she slowly brought herself back up. When I looked down a second time her head was moving rhythmically from side to side.

'Having fun Sig?' I checked again. From behind it seemed like she was coolly swaying to calypso. Trees, cars, joggers, walkers: Sigi was calmly taking in everything around her. After a while she stretched up further, gaining confidence as I continued to turn the pedals.

Bianca, on the other hand, wasn't doing so well. 'How's it going back there?' I checked. On the perimeter road around Regent's Park the traffic had become heavier. I could hear the tempo of Bianca's voice raise as she became flustered.

'Yeah, I'm okay. But what gear do I need now?' she called out.

'What gear are you in?' I yelled.

'I have no idea!'

I realized this was going to take time. In my mind I filed Bianca's cycling under 'work in progress'.

Somehow we managed to make it round and ended up stopping for a rest by Queen Mary's Garden in the heart of the park, apparently the largest collection of roses in the whole of London. Though at that time of year the winter beds were sadly bare. When I'd first cycled through in the summer, gold, red, pink and pale yellow petals unfurled towards the sun and roses twisted around its pergolas. Gardeners were out in force tending them alongside visitors ambling through or sprawled out on the nearby grass. Now the boating lake on its far side was almost silent, other than the cries of a couple of seagulls and swans. Sigi got preoccupied exploring the ornate water fountain now trickling ice-cold water. She seemed the most blissed out of all of us. *Can we swap places?* I thought.

The basket had done its job well, but if Sigi was going to come out again then there was another aspect to consider. What if she needed to go to the toilet? On shorter rides, it hadn't seemed to bother her. Usually Sigi gets restless if she needs to use her litter tray at home. But if we were to travel further it could become an issue. When I googled around, the best option seemed to be lining it with puppy training pads – soft, absorbent squares of material that she could sit on and pee without having to get out or become distressed. The next time we headed out she took to it immediately as I lifted her in, the lining having the added benefit of being a softer bed to move around on than the scratchy canvas.

On that occasion, we took a detour from Regent's Park along the canal, behind its famous zoo, all the way to Camden Town. Ever since I'd come to London I'd been fascinated by the area – a bohemian enclave where you can still see punks and piercing parlours and goths with their dark clothing and heavy boots strolling up the main street. At the top end, the narrow graffiti-covered hotchpotch of buildings opens out to where a labyrinth of markets overlook the canal, with stalls selling anything from hippy clothes and antiques, to old books and vinyl records. If I ever went on foot I could spend hours wandering, but like everywhere in London that December the streets were emptier and less colourful than they had been in the summer just gone.

For Sigi, though, she'd become like a cat in Disneyland. As I powered through Camden High Street I noticed that instead of her head bobbing from side to side, she had begun to focus in on specific objects. Suddenly she hunkered down, her eyes peeking over the basket's aluminium rim. Her ears flattened the way they did whenever she stalked cats and birds while sat on the ledge in the study.

'What you looking at Sig?' When I followed her head she'd set her sights on a flock of pigeons pecking crumbs by the side of the road. In a flash, one spread its wings and dived in from the side, flapping haphazardly within touching distance. Crouched down and ready to pounce, Sigi went into full stealth mode but the pigeon turned abruptly and swooped across her head before flying off. She craned her neck backwards and watched it disappear from view.

'You almost got that one Sigi!' I shouted to her. That was the first moment I also realized that with Sigi moving around so abruptly, I needed to take extra care to steady my bike and stop it from wobbling.

Days later we cycled further to an area called Nine Elms on the south bank of the River Thames and made our way along one of London's cycle superhighways: narrow, blue-painted tracks that separate bikes from traffic and link the suburbs to the city centre. I'd used them a couple of times in the summer and found that I could pick up a good speed. *How would Sigi react if I stepped up the pace?* I wondered.

As I pushed on, she hauled herself up and rested her paws on the basket edge, stretching out her back like the lookout on a ship's bridge. I felt a pang of nostalgia as memories of Sigi as a kitten flooded my mind. Sigi was scanning the horizon in exactly the same way she'd done when she was three months old, climbing up on the steering wheel and then the dashboard on the journey home from Hermosa Beach, letting the vibration of the engine pulse through her. Now, when the Garmin registered a steady 20mph she stretched up higher, taking in the silver cube of the newly built American Embassy, with its futuristic, curving, metallic plates reflected in the river.

'Wave to home,' I told her, trying to make light of our precarious visa situation.

By the time we reached the criss-cross of intersections at Vauxhall Bridge, Sigi was leaning into the wind and letting it flutter through her hair. Whenever I slowed down or stopped, she turned her head and stared at me questioningly: *Hey, what you doing, buddy? Where's the fun gone?* When I got going again, she turned and resumed her figurehead position.

'You like some speed, huh?' I asked. I'd had a funny feeling Sigi would but now I was concerned about the cold. I'd dressed her that morning in a red woollen sweater, but as we cycled on, the tips of my fingers had become red and raw. I pulled my cycling gloves down. Would she let me know if she was uncomfortable? I decided to brave it so long as she could. The longer we cycled, the longer I wanted to stay outdoors.

Strangely, over the next few weeks I felt myself getting back into a routine. Every afternoon when we got home my body tingled with energy. I was beginning to feel more alive than I had done in months. At times on the road I also found myself working through my situation, trying to put life in perspective. Sometimes I felt lucky to be alive. The pandemic had robbed so many people of their lives. The death toll – well over a hundred thousand by now – was bleak and sobering. But in other moments I felt hopeless in my small world. So far, none of my job applications had been successful. Having no income terrified me. I'd already started to dip into my savings and I found myself obsessively checking my account, watching it tick down. Bianca's work visa was still stalling and the threat of being removed remained over us. Although bizarrely, given our situation, around this time I also stopped looking for work.

Maybe I was still processing losing my job for the umpteenth time. When I thought about it, that word 'capable' that my father had always used stabbed at me like a dart. If I wasn't working, was I capable? Or was I useless? Or worthless? Yet being out with Sigi was gradually opening my eyes to something, even though I wasn't sure what. Another way of existing maybe? A life that wasn't regulated by clocks or managers or markets or global pandemics – a life that felt freer than any stagnant office job and a diary full of deadlines. Now instead of opening up my emails after I'd grabbed my morning coffee, I found myself staring at Google Maps.

'Where are we going today?' I asked Sigi as she hopped up on the desk and sat with me in front of the screen. As well as choosing routes that I might enjoy, I found myself thinking about what Sigi would like to see. To outsiders that probably sounds super-weird, but discovering a city at random with a willing travelling partner is something maybe I'd always been attracted to. I'd just never had the opportunity. Growing up, I'd loved the writings of the American Beat Generation: Allen Ginsberg and William S Burroughs, and Jack Kerouac's classic novel *On the Road* in particular drew me in. Its protagonist Sal Paradise left post-war New York City where everything felt dead, throwing away alarm clocks and timetables and all the trappings of a nine-to-five and grifting through the towns of the American West with his companion Dean Moriarty. Often I'd dreamed about being like Sal, taking chances, meeting strangers and opening myself up to new experiences – a search for freedom where the journey mattered far more than the destination.

Every day when Sigi and I got home, I'd also got into a routine of editing down any video I'd taken that day and uploading it to my Instagram account. I found that process as meditative as cycling itself: running through the footage, watching Sigi's reaction to the world around her fascinated me. What I hadn't expected was that it had started to fascinate others too.

After I posted the video of Sigi pouncing at the pigeon I woke up to find 500 new followers on my Instagram account. *Are these bots?* The thought did cross my mind. I couldn't imagine real people had found my page and wanted to view it. My handle name was Skintension after a song by Man Man – an obscure, experimental LA band that I loved. Was it that or a cat that had sent people there? Besides, in the early days of posting I didn't use any special tags other than a nod to my bike with the hashtag #fixedgear. My reasoning? Like anywhere in the world, the fixed-gear community is niche and maybe I could reach out to it in London. I followed enough couriers and professional riders and I'd enjoyed running into Mat that day in Marylebone, although I hadn't seen him since. Maybe subconsciously not being in a young start-up had also deprived me of being around energetic, like-minded people and I wanted to connect.

Christmas came and went without much of a bang, other than a few drinks that week with Lexi and Mary and a quiet day phoning friends and family. But as the new year rolled in, me and Sigi set out on the road again. Since I'd bought my bike I'd been clocking up impressive mileage on my Strava account, but now Sigi had become my regular sidekick I thought it would be fun if she had one too. That month Sigi got her own personal Strava and I began posting her stats online.

Since my initial posts in mid-December I'd also gained a few extra Instagram followers and visitors to my page had started commenting, confirming to me that these were *actual* followers. Some asked about how Sigi coped with the noise of the traffic, not knowing she was deaf, and more people tuned in to say how brilliant seeing Sigi was. Others just expressed themselves with heart-shaped emojis. *Wow, people are genuinely interested,* I thought. Mostly I was still intrigued at how followers were finding me, so I began experimenting with a few extra hashtags. Alongside #fixedgear, I posted #norwegianforestcat – another very niche community. Then #cyclist, #cyclinglife, and then by area #northlondon and #belsizepark. As much as I enjoyed making and posting videos, the responses had also sparked the data analyst in me. Every day I became preoccupied with the numbers of people logging on to view Sigi in her basket riding through London's streets, even if the footage was far from skilled.

That month we travelled out to Queen Elizabeth Olympic Park where the London 2012 Olympic Games had been held. My lone cycles along the Lea Valley in the summer had been a great adventure and the park sits at the foot of it. Being into sports I'd remembered watching much of those Olympics from my sofa in San Francisco. Now stood up next to the stadium, I couldn't help thinking how much smaller it looked – like so many of London's landmarks such as Big Ben or Buckingham Palace. As we made our way around its outer edge and along the wilderness trails to the velodrome and beyond, the thunder clouds rolled in and the rain began to spit. Quickly, I snapped a picture of Sigi next to the five Olympic rings and headed back, making another note to experiment with a way to shelter her. On the ride back she hunkered down in the basket, at times trying to keep dry under the excess material lining its sides while I let the wet completely drench me. It felt so refreshing.

A few days later we cycled into town and ended up weaving in and out of the lattice of Victorian streets around Covent Garden. Every lane we turned down felt like a new adventure and as my tyres bumped over the neatly cobbled stones, I creased up laughing as Sigi's head juddered up and down like a pneumatic drill. It didn't seem to bother her at all. On that trip we discovered Neal's Yard – a secret courtyard behind the main drag, filled with independent restaurants and boutiques. We rested there for a while and people-watched while Sigi drew in a small crowd of passers-by, keen to give her a stroke. On the way home we detoured through Leicester Square where Sigi resumed her new hobby of pigeon hunting. They tormented her and she ducked and dived around the basket as the birds fanned up from the pavement and flew clumsily overhead.

One day I waited until it got dark before taking Sigi out on her first night ride. 'Want to see some bright lights?' I asked her. Whenever Bianca and I had been to the theatre before the pandemic I'd loved the wall of neon advertising signs at Piccadilly Circus, especially it's all-American Coca-Cola hoarding flashing and moving like a miniature Times Square or the Las Vegas Strip. I'd also read some studies that suggested deaf cats have better-developed peripheral vision than those who can hear. They are supposed to be tuned in to following motion. A night ride could be an opportunity to test that out. Being nocturnal, Sigi was also wide awake most evenings. Bianca accompanied us for some extra practise. She'd been out a few more times and I could see her courage growing as Sigi and I cruised behind her. The blue and red flashing lights of an ambulance had Sigi hypnotized, as did the succession of car tail lights passing us.

'Hey Sig, look, there's Eros.' I tapped her head as we drifted into Piccadilly Circus and stopped briefly at its famous fountain. Although the statue is known as Eros it isn't Eros at all, I discovered, but his twin brother Anteros – the Greek god of requited love – pointing his bow and arrow. Sigi nodded approvingly before gazing up at the wall of light radiating from the digital advertising screens.

In fact, I sensed that Sigi loved being out in the dark more than she did any other time. A few days later when we stumbled across Leake Street Arches– a long underground tunnel beneath Waterloo Station on the south side of the River Thames – she appeared to come alive. I felt a rush of excitement too. Who would have guessed that running directly under the multitude of train platforms would be an artists' paradise? When I read up on it later, I learned it's the one place in London where graffiti is legal and it's nicknamed the 'Banksy Tunnel' after the famous street artist. The illusive artist used it for a secret event back in 2008 to celebrate artists from around the world and since then it has become a Mecca, its walls and ceilings changing week by week as new tags and images get spray-painted on.

'Super-cool, hey Sig?' I slowed down so we could both take it in. Sigi carefully followed the patterns covering the walls and her head craned upwards along the arc of the tunnel's roof. She looked searchingly at the brightly coloured murals: faces, animals, words, abstract drawings – a visual assault on the senses that had us both hooked. When I looked over a quiet contentment had spread across her face. I tickled her neck and leaned in to give her a kiss. *What do you think about when you're out with me?* I wondered. Our rides were doing me the power of good. I only hoped she felt the same.

10

PROTECTOR OF THE REALM

So far Sigi and I had been experiencing London at road level, but in March 2021 it was time to turn up the heat. That month, I began keeping a comprehensive list of ideas of where we could travel and or fun things we could do together. I'd spotted the cable car across the River Thames on Google Maps when Sigi and I had first visited the Olympic Park and wanted to revisit the area. It is a little further south and takes visitors between the Royal Docks and the Greenwich Peninsula, where we could explore The O2 – the huge entertainment venue that sits on the water's edge. Formerly named the Millennium Dome, it was built originally as an exhibition space to usher in the millennium in 2000. How Sigi would react to being suspended 90 metres above London's East End was anyone's guess. According to one website, that's the height of 20 double-decker buses stacked on top of each other. If Sigi suffered from vertigo, I'd soon find out.

That day we set off around mid-morning. I planned to tackle the sky ride from the Greenwich side. From Primrose

Hill, we cycled down through Regent's Park to Hyde Park then past Buckingham Palace and The Mall until we hit the Thames Path on the south side of the river and wound our way to Greenwich.

Numerous cyclists were out that day and several turned their heads as they passed to give us the thumbs-up. As I hit one red light on the perimeter of Regent's Park, a courier who had waved at us earlier pulled up for a chat.

'Beautiful cat. Does she like the basket?' he asked.

'Seems to love it!' I replied as he got his phone out to take a picture.

'Do you take her out often?'

I looked down at the screen strapped to my handlebars and read Sigi's Strava recording. 'So far this year we've done a hundred and fifty miles together,' I said proudly. The moment I said it I realized how much we'd increased our mileage in just two months.

'Nice one!' he shouted before the lights turned green and he blasted off.

I'd calculated the trip would take around three hours – one of the longest routes we'd taken so far. Again, another experiment. On our trips I noticed that Sigi got restless after an hour or so. She would circle around in the basket or try to climb out. Normally, when that happened I took her out on the leash to stretch her legs. In those early days, she would never curl up and sleep if she was tired, curiosity always got the better of her. Like me, she suffers the worst FOMO – an almost pathological fear of missing out. *Like father like cat,* I thought.

As we approached the cable car Sigi's eyes followed the flight line.

'That's where we're headed!' I pointed up. I hadn't even checked whether cats were permitted on the cable car, but as we entered the ticket hall that apprehension disappeared. There was nothing but smiles from the attendants.

'Oh wow! A cat?' One woman stretched over and gave Sigi a pat before I swiped my phone on the sensor. Because of Covid-19, we'd have a cable car all to ourselves, she explained.

'Her very own carriage,' I joked, rolling my eyes. Princess Sigi seemed to be loving this pampering and pressed her nose against each mobile screen as a couple more staff drifted over to take her picture.

'Have fun!' the attendant shouted as we disappeared into the lift.

Just so Sigi could enjoy the full panoramic experience, I let her out on her leash to climb around. After giving the upholstery a good look-over she hopped up and took her seat as if looking down from the balcony of her very own theatre. As it turned out, I had less of a head for heights than Sigi. Slowly we glided up.

Ker-clunk. The noise of the grip clicking over the first tower signalled we'd reached maximum height. Below us a web of roads weaved in and out and the river snaked in a horseshoe around a peninsula called the Isle of Dogs. 'You'd hate it there,' I teased Sigi as she turned her face in disgust and gazed in the other direction. No one is sure why it's named the Isle of Dogs but one theory is it was originally marshland and called the Isle of Ducks given it was home to a community of wildfowl and the name changed over time.

'Hey look!' I tapped Sigi. I could see sunlight gleaming off something in the other direction. When I looked closer, it was the Thames Barrier. I'd only ever seen it in pictures before, but the structure looked like steel armadillos lined up to defend the city. It's one of the world's largest flood barriers. Looking back westwards I spotted the distinctive dome of St Paul's Cathedral and the skyscrapers of London's financial district rising up like glass obelisks.

'The ride's over Sig,' I announced as we drifted down to the north bank. It was clear Sigi did not want to leave. In the end I had to scoop her up off the seat and place her in the basket ready to begin the next leg of our ride.

Later that afternoon I uploaded my edited-down video to Instagram. This time, I also posted a longer video of the ride along the Thames Path on YouTube, just to see if it got any traction. With a growing number of followers each day, I debated whether I should improve my footage even though there was something do-it-yourself and amateur about it that I liked. *However, if people were tuning in to see Sigi they deserved some professionalism,* I thought. The perfectionist in me also loved to tinker. That evening I ordered up a cheap selfie stick from Amazon.

The next time Sigi and I rode out I played around with the selfie stick. On one of the quieter pathways in Regent's Park I cycled up and down with the GoPro attached, holding it out with my hand. In my mind I wanted to capture a unique view of Sigi and have footage that felt far more streamlined than what I'd been able to achieve with the shaky handlebar attachment I'd used so far. After grabbing several shots from the side, above and in front, I headed home and uploaded it with Sigi watching on. Out front with a side-on view of Sigi jumped out as the most dramatic angle. It captured her like a dream – *Kind of iconic*, I thought. Securing the stick to the handlebars with two hose clips also worked perfectly.

The next day, we made our way into town. So far, other than keeping my speed steady and avoiding heavy traffic, I'd not considered many safety issues around Sigi. Up until this point, everyone who'd waved at us or called out did so with a smile or a look of bewilderment as if to say: *Seriously? Has a cat in a basket just flown by?* On this particular day, having made our way from Regent's Park to Hyde Park, we hit Constitution Hill to the west of Buckingham Palace – apparently a famous spot for duels hundreds of years ago. I loved it less for its history and more because the roads there had zero potholes, unlike so many others on our routes. Mainly I swerved around them, but when you have a cat on board and there's heavy traffic, pulling out feels precarious and we thumped over them.

As we cycled on past Green Park, clumps of daffodils had started to flower. I felt a curious mix of emotions. Six months ago I'd barely been able to lift myself off the sofa. I'd been the victim of something beyond my control, feeling hard done by and turned inside out. Now I slowed down to admire anything that resembled a fresh start. Early spring in London is when the trees outside our apartment burst into life again and patches of crocuses popped all over the city's green spaces. Along The

Mall flags billowed in the breeze as Admiralty Arch loomed into view. Just as I was approaching I spotted a woman lurching up the roadside towards us. She had on a bobble hat and a large coat. At first she stared at Sigi, then at me. I smiled and slowed down. Maybe she wanted to admire Sigi and give her a stroke?

Suddenly she spun her head around to face us. Her eyes were alight with rage and she snarled up her lip and spat. *Eueeewwww, that sucks!* I thought. A large globule of sputum narrowly missed Sigi and dribbled down the bike frame. It all happened so quickly that I was slow to react. *Did that just happen?* Nothing that disgusting had ever happened to us.

'Hey Sig. You okay?' I checked concernedly. Sigi had craned her neck back and was scowling at the woman. The encounter dumbfounded me. *Is she crazy? Does she have a problem with cyclists or with Sigi?* I couldn't work it out at all.

At the moment I turned around to shout at her I noticed the bright blue and yellow markings of a police car waiting in the queue of traffic opposite. I wasted no time in cycling over and rapping on the window. 'Hey, did you see that? That woman just spat on me and my cat!' I told the two officers as the window glided down.

'Where did it land?' one officer nursing a takeaway coffee said. I noticed him staring perplexed at Sigi.

'On my bike, but we're in a pandemic!' I said. Inside the anger was stinging.

'Did it get on your face?' the other officer interrupted.

'I don't think so, but spitting is a crime isn't it?' I was becoming frustrated at how little interest they were showing.

'So long as it didn't get on your face,' the officer said before the lights changed and the window glided back up.

Jesus Christ! I thought. If they'd shown any interest that woman could have been arrested there and then.

After that I abandoned our ride altogether. Maybe the woman was crazy, but the incident felt very personal. As I pushed up Haverstock Hill it ran circles around my mind. During Covid there had been far fewer people to meet, but so far all my interactions had been positive. Sigi distracted people and made them laugh. When I thought about it, I also loved that she made people happy. Every time they pointed or smiled or came to pat her it gave me a feeling of warmth. However hard, I couldn't let this catapult me back to square one, but the incident made me realize I still felt very fragile.

That afternoon when I fast-forwarded through my video, I replayed the scene over and over. What irritated me more than anything was the police's nonchalance, so much so that a few hours later I put in a call. The incident had been filed, I was told. Apparently the woman had been causing trouble elsewhere, yet I still couldn't help thinking her bile was aimed at us. *What if I stumbled across similar random people who hated us as much?* I worried.

I toyed with posting up my video. Maybe it was a bit ugly? A woman spitting on a cat probably won't make prime-time viewing. Maybe a whole bunch of people landed on my page for escapism? Maybe they didn't want to see reality? But the thought sparked a deeper question: what exactly did I want my videos to show? Was I a guy who wanted to sugar-coat the world and pretend that bad shit didn't happen? Or should Sigi and I seek out interesting stuff – maybe stuff even we didn't understand and show it to our audience? Maybe stuff that was uncomfortable at times? Certainly the latter would be truer to myself and more fascinating. *Embrace it, Travis,* I thought.

While editing the video I experimented with the slow-mo function on the software, slowing the footage down at precisely the moment the woman spat to give it extra effect. Later when I checked my Instagram there was confirmation that I'd been right to upload it. A small army of people had posted their disgust. Surprisingly, one woman had also private-messaged me. She owned a restaurant in Central London and had been spat on by the same woman. *Don't worry, she's nuts,* she told me. Immediately it put me at ease – far more than the phone call to the police had. One of the best comments read: *What is wrong with people? Loving this cam angle!* Hilarious that an eagle-eyed follower had noticed the new selfie stick angle. I'd almost forgotten about it in all the drama. It did look super-cool. I closed my laptop and called it a day. *Not everyone's going to love you Travis, but keep going,* I thought.

A few weeks later another strange incident happened. I woke to find a message from a clothing company called Adapt Clothing that I'd regularly bought from in San Francisco. From our flat in the Sunset District, its flagship store was only one block down. On the day the woman spat at me I'd been wearing one of their hats with the word 'Misfit' sewn into the front – the nickname for the San Francisco Giants American football team. On another video a gust of wind had blown my hat off and I'd had to retrieve it from the roadside. *Hey, we noticed you wearing us. Want a new hat?* the message read. Wow. So far, I'd guessed it was only Sigi lovers who followed us. I was surprised to find a brand tuning in too. *How did you find me?* I asked. Apparently a customer who followed my Instagram had sent them a link.

When a new hat arrived days later with a selection of stickers, it felt unnerving. This was a store I hadn't set eyes on in 18 months, but they found me over 5,000 miles away. As I opened up the package and emptied out its contents, a longing for home overwhelmed me. My mind began spinning. *Maybe we can't stay here? Maybe when the pandemic is over we'll get thrown out anyway, we'll go home and I'll get another nine-to-five.* Jesus, a nine-to-five. I needed that like a hole in the head. But I also needed to face facts. What had started in London as an adventure hadn't gone to plan. Now Sigi and I were travelling aimlessly around a city without any real purpose. Sooner or later I was going to run out of money. The negative thoughts had returned full force. *Just call it a day Travis and go home.* I turned the scenario over in my mind and decided to sleep on it.

The next day, however, another message pinged up. When I clicked on it, I scanned down in disbelief. The digital media company The Dodo had also been viewing my clips. *Wow, this is wild.* Every committed animal lover knows about The Dodo – a monthly audience of 110 million in the US alone across social media platforms and its website which features daily stories about pets and animals. One traveller who I'd occasionally followed on the site was Dean Nicholson, who found his cat Nala on a roadside in Bosnia while cycling around the world. She'd become his companion for the whole journey and he'd recorded their adventures on Instagram. It was only through The Dodo finding his page that his story ever reached a wider audience.

We noticed your page and wondered if you'd be interested in sharing clips of you and Sigrid on our website, a message from Indiana, its digital content manager, read. After a little toing and froing she offered to pay me a small fee to license my clips.

Agreed, I wrote back without hesitation. In fact, it felt exhilarating. Once again it was as if this vast digital universe reached out and pulled me in a different direction every time my self-esteem took a hit. Over the next few months the arrangement did stall due to problems caused by the pandemic at The Dodo's head office, but the approach gave me a real boost.

In some ways the interactions with Sigi and I felt like occasions when I was back in San Francisco. Whenever I took my Chevy Nova out on the road, passers-by gave me so much love. I could see their eyes glazing over with a hazy sentimentality. 'We owned one of these when I was younger. Haven't seen this beauty in a while,' became a regular comment. Drivers would stop at traffic lights, lean out of the window and holler over or give me an enthusiastic thumbs-up. Or an aficionado would wander over at a gas station and run their hand along its chassis: 'Lovely car you've got there,' they'd say beaming.

But what was it about Sigi and I that viewers loved? I wondered. Over that month, I decided to track my followers to see if I could find any clues. Mostly, I figured they'd be from

London. People might recognize the landmarks of their home town and want to follow us. Maybe watching inspired them to get out and cycle themselves now the winter was over and lockdown lifting soon was pretty much a certainty. Surely, at the very furthest, followers would be living around the UK – checking in from cities like Birmingham or Manchester or smaller towns and villages. Maybe they'd lived in London once and enjoyed the nostalgia hit? But when I ran some analytics I was taken aback. Only a quarter of my followers had a URL registered in London and the UK. Another quarter were coming to my site from the US. Others logged in from mainland Europe. In the Middle East I especially had followers in Turkey, where apparently cats are revered, and there was a percentage from South East Asia, in particular Indonesia. Weird, but true. Without trying, I was amassing an international audience who only had eyes for Sigi. What was even stranger was that I knew nothing about them whatsoever. With this growing fanbase I added a few more hashtags to my posts – all the words I could find that translated to the word cat : #gatos #michi #pishi #kot #kit #chat #kedi #katze #gatto #katt #貓 #ネコ #고양이 #kucing

As March rolled into April, Sigi and I rode out more, often with Bianca joining us. Although I was cycling to many of our go-to places, I also found myself gravitating to unusual sights. Just like Sigi was honing in on pigeons and passers-by, I was noticing people – tiny subcultures that popped up in different parts of the city. One day I'd cycled out alone and came across a whole bunch of kids riding their bikes along the Thames Embankment. These weren't fixed-gear riders. Instead their bikes looked like customized mountain bikes. Around 30 were spinning and skidding and doing wheelies down an empty stretch of road – an urban peloton of mainly boys in beanie hats and hoodies. Around me I could hear chains whizzing as they shouted and whooped. I joined for a stretch before I spotted a police riot van in the distance and a couple of officers hovering on the pavement ready to pull them over. Later, when I searched online to find out who they were, I didn't find a small group but a whole movement. Under the hashtag #bikelife I read about a community of riders, mainly from disaffected backgrounds, using cycling as a way to express themselves – not that the authorities saw it that way. Apparently a task force of police had been mounted to tackle what it saw as a threat on the streets, but in the short time I'd tagged along, I hadn't sensed any sinister vibe at all – just kids riding together and showing off their skills.

Then one Saturday morning towards the end of the month when Bianca, Sigi and I headed into town we were faced with another unexpected crowd. As we made our way through Hyde Park I could see hordes of people up ahead streaming in through the steel gates around Hyde Park Corner. Immediately I knew this would freak Bianca out.

'There's too many people, Travis,' she hollered from behind. Even in the open air Bianca felt more nervous than I did about Covid-19 and still wore her mask while out cycling.

'Nah, it's fine. Let's see who they are. We'll push through,' I reassured her. To this day, Bianca jokes that I'm too nosey for my own good.

However, as we got closer I could feel the atmosphere becoming charged. A few thousand unmasked people were marching, many brandishing banners. The red smoke of flares hung in the air. When I peered in further some of the banners read:

END THE LOCKDOWN

NO TO VACCINE PASSPORTS

GIVE FLU A CHANCE

With swarms of people now around us, my stomach lurched. Fresh in my mind was the woman who'd spat at Sigi and I feared that this crowd may be as hostile. I'd only seen news reports of the anti-vax movement on Twitter and it didn't look too friendly, but I'd never stumbled across an actual march before. Bianca and I had received our first vaccines, so it wasn't a cause I felt too much sympathy with. *Even so, everyone has a right to protest,* I thought.

'I'll get you out of here,' I said to Sigi, realizing my mistake and stretching down to give her a soothing scratch to the back of her neck. Sigi had never been in a sea of protesters before. Was she frightened? Her head swayed as normal. She seemed to be calmly taking in the onslaught of people, but I felt seriously on edge. Unable to make any headway, I got off my bike and Bianca did the same. We'd have to weave our way through on foot. This panicked me. Although Sigi was attached to the basket by her leash, a million thoughts ran through my head: *What if someone tries to snatch her? Or hurt her?* Desperate to get to the roadside I pushed on, clutching the back of her harness with one hand and steering my bike with the other.

'I don't like this Travis,' Bianca called out. I agreed. Some marchers were casually chatting as they walked, but others wore angry scowls and were shouting. Through the gaps I could see the uniforms and helmets of police circling on the sidelines. I had an awful feeling that if anything kicked off, we'd find ourselves at the centre of erupting violence. *Relax, Travis,* I told myself, taking a deep breath. As soon as I did, something weird happened. When I looked up, the faces etched with frowns began to soften. Instead I found myself focusing in on smiles and eyes staring adoringly at Sigi.

'Oh look at this cat!' One woman headed straight towards us. 'Can I stroke her?' she asked.

'Erm . . . sure,' I said cautiously. Part of me just wanted to get the hell out of there. My fingers tightened around Sigi's harness.

'Come over, look at this cat,' the woman shouted to her friend. Now a small group gathered to give Sigi a stroke and ask me what breed she was.

'She's a Norwegian Forest cat,' I replied.

'She's a brave cat in all these people,' another woman commented.

'Oh she's deaf,' I explained.

'Really? I've never met a deaf cat!' She gazed up at me in amazement.

Sigi didn't seem to mind the attention and even posed for a

few selfies with some of the marchers. To her, everyone was equal regardless of their views. She was right, of course. I wasn't an anti-vaxxer, but maybe I'd been too quick to judge? When Bianca and I emerged from the crowd we were completely unscathed. We jumped back on our bikes and headed towards Piccadilly Circus.

That evening, I found myself reflecting on the afternoon. Taking Sigi through the anti-vax protest had given me an added confidence that maybe I could take her out to larger gatherings. As the lockdowns were easing I felt the need to get out and mingle too. That said, I was anxious not to overexpose Sigi or put her in a situation where she could become an easy target. Back in the US, I'd joined in protests for issues that were close to my heart. Like most Americans, the right to free speech was one of those issues, and I hated any heavy-handed attempts at state control. At home, though, protests sometimes turned ugly. There's an element called the Black Bloc – violent anarchist extremists who often turn up dressed in balaclavas on a mission to destroy everything. That's always my cue for a sharp exit. Easy enough when it's only me, but Sigi was hardly the nimblest vigilante. I'd never be able to forgive myself if she got accidentally hit by a brick or a police truncheon or sprayed with tear gas. In the UK maybe that was a remote possibility but I had to consider every eventuality with my new travelling buddy. Yet at the anti-vax protests Sigi had become a quiet, calming force. 'You're not exactly Mahatma Gandhi, but you are a little peacemaker,' I said, giving her a back rub as she hopped up on to my lap.

Not long after, posts started coming through my Facebook

feed about an upcoming march in Central London. This time people would be protesting about a bill going through Parliament that limited the public's right to protest. I'd always looked suspiciously at police cracking down on protest – even in situations where people fling themselves on top of subway trains or chain themselves to motorway bridges for their cause – but the idea that police could just stop people for being loud or a little wild while ultimately peacefully protesting in a democratic country was a step too far in my view. Wherever in the world that was happening, it was the type of overreach that felt troubling to me. And if people's right to protest gets watered down so much then you may as well join a Thanksgiving parade. I wanted to show my support.

'Hey Sig, want to help me defend democracy?' I fooled around with her that morning as I got my cycling gear ready. Sigi looked up hopefully but I sensed some caution: *Sure, I'll be your mascot. Just don't ask me to glue my paws to the Houses of Parliament.*

'I got this for you,' I said, holding up the newest outfit I'd found for her. If Sigi was going to be a protector of the realm she should at least look slightly intimidating. Online I'd spotted a 'tactical vest' worn by military dogs in combat situations – black Cordura with proper buckles that was also flame retardant. Some vests in the range had ballistics panels. For sure, protests could get fraught but I doubted she'd need protection from being shot at. Instead I opted for a cheaper, simpler version with Velcro pads to attach what the military calls 'morale patches' – embroidered messages like 'No Mercy' or 'One Size Kills All'. I clicked on one that read 'Beast Mode'. Perfect. *That should repel any threat,* I thought.

'What do you think?' Sigi looked up, giving me a concerned look. 'Not your style?' I asked, attaching it around her torso. Sigi turned her head in feigned disgust. 'Okay, have it your way,' I conceded, fishing out a pink and yellow Hawaiian bandana I already had in Sigi's wardrobe. I tied it around her neck. The ensemble didn't quite hang together but Sigi seemed happy. *Talk about sending out mixed messages,* I laughed to myself.

The march started at Trafalgar Square and would snake its way down The Mall and loop back towards Westminster. If we got there bang on midday then we could avoid the large crowds that might gather later. In advance I'd planned only on taking Sigi along the wider stretches of road so we could duck out if anything kicked off, or if Sigi got restless. As we cycled through Regent's Park and made our way on down Oxford Street we could see a trickle of protesters carrying banners drifting towards the start. Edging closer towards Trafalgar Square I heard the faint beat of drums and the reverberation of voices through a loudspeaker. Far from being a hostile environment, it felt like a carnival. Compared to the States it was seriously freestyle too. There, a hardcore group of organizers usually corral people into position shouting like lieutenants through megaphones before any march begins. What surprised me in London is that people were just milling around.

'Let's go with the flow,' I said to Sigi.

Pretty soon, Sigi's military cover was completely blown. The combat jacket repelled precisely zero admirers. We'd never witnessed so many people wandering over to say hi. I got off my bike and wheeled it through Trafalgar Square but we could hardly move a few steps without someone petting Sigi. A melting pot of people of all races and nationalities and ages approached us. Some people seemed like Londoners but others were clearly tourists or foreigners living in the city like me.

'Absolutely gorgeous.' One middle-aged guy couldn't resist stroking Sigi's head and stopping for a chat.

'Oh wow, you're a little anti-facist kitten!' A woman made a beeline for Sigi and tickled her under her chin. She waved over at her friends to join her.

'What a cutie,' they cooed as they walked closer. Although people were asking me about Sigi, this was the first time I'd been out with her that I sensed that I'd become invisible. All people were interested in was her. Instead, I'd become the security detail for a celebrity on the red carpet.

At the fountains in the middle of the square, I lifted Sigi out of her basket and let her wander around on her leash for a while. On all the trips we'd done together she seemed to love dipping her nose into water or getting her paws wet. Near London Bridge Station only a few weeks earlier I'd had to prise her away from one water feature which was simple slabs of granite stone with water flowing gently over them. Sigi was mesmerized and given half the chance would have stayed there all day.

On the other side of Trafalgar Square, as we weaved our way around the famous lions guarding the foot of Nelson's Column, two police officers approached. *Here we go,* I thought. So far the atmosphere at this protest had felt upbeat, but maybe we'd outstayed our welcome. A guy with a cat *must* be doing something suspicious. Besides, I still didn't even have a legal right to be in the UK. Now Sigi and I were protesting against the government. Before I could alter direction, one of the female officers lunged at us.

With her mask obscuring her face she looked deadly serious, but within seconds I watched as her eyes lit up. 'I don't even like cats!' she giggled, unable to resist giving Sigi's head a full-bodied rub.

Saved by my cat. I exhaled and laughed nervously at the officer.

As protesters circled around, one guy called over. He was holding a camera with a very professional-looking lens. He had a determined air about him, like he was doing a job. 'Mind if I take a picture?' he asked.

'No sure, go ahead,' I agreed. As he did Sigi lifted her head up. She stared directly into the lens and then turned slightly to the side, like she was offering him her best angle. So far she'd been in the glare of mobile phone cameras, but this was a different level.

'Thanks, mate,' he called over. I'd wanted to ask him if he was working for a newspaper or whether I'd be able to find the picture online, but as soon as the shutter clicked he turned and disappeared into the crowd before I had the chance.

'Paparazzi now, huh?' I said to Sigi.

Sigi yawned and hunkered down in her basket. She could barely keep her eyes open. All the attention had exhausted her. We moved with the crowd through Admiralty Arch and down The Mall for a while longer before hitting the road home.

11

COOL FOR CATS

By late May, Sigi and I were exploring almost every day. My followers were growing and, with hindsight, I'd started to put some pressure on myself to make them happy. Although my content wasn't paying my rent, it was starting to feel like a day job – a routine we'd fallen into. As time went on I also noticed Sigi had fallen into a new routine too. Whenever she woke and she watched me collect my bike gear she padded into the kitchen to eat before mooching by the door. It made me think that maybe she got more hungry on the rides than I'd realized. I made sure a bowl of food was ready for her beforehand and took a few extra treats with me just in case.

One morning I found Sigi in the study glued to the cat superhighway. She'd seemed a little withdrawn over the previous days, although I couldn't see that she was ill. Usually if Sigi is under the weather she curls up alone and withdraws from the world. Instead, she just looked sad and seemed less playful. 'Hey Sig, where do you want to go today?' I tapped her gently on her back. At that moment Sigi's head spun around. Her four fangs flashed at me as her mouth opened wide. She thrust out her bright pink tongue and let out an almighty hiss. I jumped back. Sigi never behaved like that before a ride.

'Okay, okay,' I tried to calm her. Of course, I'd seen Sigi hiss many times but mainly at Ylva if they were fighting, or at a stranger. My heart sank. As much as I was opening Sigi's eyes to the world, she was opening mine to places and people I wouldn't meet otherwise, however fleeting. Now, though, I felt an overwhelming pang of guilt. Maybe I was being selfish? Maybe I needed to be more mindful of Sigi's needs? Had I been expecting her to accompany me every time partly so we could please our growing number of fans? With new followers our lives were changing. People were visiting and revisiting my page for their Sigi hit. Some messages had been amazing and I felt genuinely touched by them. Notes like: *Thank you for spreading joy! Your cat is very lovely.* And: *Thanks for sharing. It puts a smile to my day!* Subconsciously, though, I realized I'd been stressing out about how much content I needed to upload knowing that people were relying on us.

When I considered it, I recognized how crazy it was to think like that. There and then I decided that it didn't matter what I wanted, or what followers wanted. If I really cared about Sigi then her welfare must come first. Her online star might be rising, but I wasn't going to act like a cruel promoter pushing her out into the limelight. If people wanted to see her, from now on it would be on her terms. Anyhow, I figured if my followers were animal lovers, as I was sure they were, they'd understand.

That day I headed out on my own. Sure enough, the ride did feel empty. I found myself looking down at the basket expecting Sigi to be there. I missed chatting to her and pointing out new sights and I also missed looking out for her. Mostly, it hit me how Sigi had become my passport to meeting people. On this ride I talked to no one. No one was interested in a guy cycling on his own. As I rode on it dawned on me how much being with Sigi had made me feel less remote and more engaged with a world I'd felt chewed up and spat out by. More human, I guess.

Thankfully it didn't take long for Sigi to perk up, and before too long we ventured out – on her terms. On the road, we were starting to recognize a greater number of people too. In early June we bumped into Mat again, this time on Hampstead Heath in North London, not far from home. I'd gotten to love the park's sprawling wilderness, especially now summer was in the air, and Sigi loved play-hunting in the long grass. Mat and I had been messaging each other a little online since our meeting in Marylebone, but it was great to connect with him in the flesh. We stumbled across each other completely by accident.

'Hey man, how you been?' I called over as soon as I saw him.

On Hampstead Heath cyclists are not allowed to ride their bikes on certain paths so he was easy to spot pushing his bike in front while looking confusedly at his phone.

'Hey! Yeah good, thanks. Don't come up this far north usually,' he shouted back. 'The hills are a killer.'

'Tell me about it,' I laughed.

Mat had to deliver a package to someone who lived in one of the multimillion-pound homes that surround the park, often hidden away behind tall security gates and long driveways. Only he couldn't find the house and it was making him late for his next delivery.

'Want some help?' I offered.

'Sure!'

He and I ended up cycling around together for half an hour before he finally made his drop and headed back into Central London.

Through my #fixedgear hashtags others from the fixed-gear scene were also discovering me online and showing an interest. A few days later Sigi and I went to Brompton Cemetery in West London, and afterwards a guy called Olivier dropped me a line. The cemetery had been on my list of places of interest. It's one of seven large cemeteries dotted around London that were built during the Victorian era, named the city's 'Magnificent Seven'. It looked like it had some great Gothic monuments and tombstones to discover, including that of the famous suffragette Emmeline Pankhurst. Just as we were cycling through I'd noticed a guy resting against his bike, with a radio – obviously a courier like Mat. But it was his cycling cap that really caught my eye. It was white with the words 'Eddy Merckx' sewn into the front.

'Hey, nice cap man, I've got the same,' I shouted over at him. Eddy Merckx is a Belgian track and road cyclist who I'd started following when I lived in Brussels – nothing less than a god in cycling circles.

'Oh cool, thanks!' He gazed up.

'You working?'

'Yup, busy!' He rolled his eyes pointing at his carrier bulging with parcels. We chatted for a while before exchanging Instagram handles. His name was Sam, and I didn't think much about the encounter until Olivier messaged me the next day saying he'd seen Sigi and I in a video Sam posted online that I'd been tagged into.

'I see you were riding fixed-gear with a cat!' Olivier said. After some back and forth he asked if we wanted to meet up. Olivier was French but living in London and was keen to meet other fixed-gear riders, he said.

'Sure,' I replied, explaining that I was in the same situation.

At the end of that week we hooked up in Trafalgar Square and rode together. We talked about bikes and living in the city before going our separate ways. Olivier was in London with his girlfriend Nadine, and we agreed to keep in touch online and meet again sometime.

After the visit to Brompton Cemetery I was keen to go back to West London. So far it was the furthest we'd travelled in that direction. Portobello Road in Notting Hill looked like an interesting adventure – a unique street in London with houses painted every colour of the rainbow and a famous market filled with stalls selling antiques, street food and vintage clothing. Naturally as soon as we arrived there, Sigi's eyes began darting around as we made our way through the streets of Notting Hill. Stallholders gave her a ton of attention too. My curiosity also got the better of me and I became intrigued by the elegant crescent-shaped terraces running off the main drag as well as being drawn in by the vibrancy and the energy of the market.

In the end, I was glad that we'd made the effort to reach Portobello Road as that morning I'd debated going out at all. As Sigi and I left home, a strong gust of wind had almost taken us off the bike. Although Portobello Road felt sheltered in a dip, I wasn't looking forward to the ride home. Dark storm clouds usually prompted me to turn around, but the wind whipping up posed another problem. Mostly Sigi loved it, but on super-blustery days she turned to face me instead of perching on the basket. Not great for our Instagram clips but crucially not great for Sigi's enjoyment. The wind was stopping her from experiencing new things.

After searching online later that evening, I decided to experiment. I remembered I'd seen a cat exactly like Sigi wearing ski goggles. A while ago a follower had tagged me into the cat's site and it didn't take long for me to find it again. Gary was a domestic long-haired cat who lived in Canada with his owner James. He had his own sizeable online following. He'd been a rescue cat before James nurtured him back to health and he turned out to be a real daredevil. There were so many awesome pictures of Gary mountaineering in the Rockies, kayaking, paddleboarding and even skiing – all wearing the funkiest goggles. Sigi had got used to most outfits I dressed her in. Maybe goggles wouldn't feel so alien? She could wear them if it was windy but also if she was facing direct sunshine. I'd often worried about how sensitive her blue eyes were to bright light. I should protect them. I ordered up a pair.

Sigi's basket was also ready to give up the ghost and it had been on my to-do list to source another more robust substitute.

As we'd been cruising around I could see it sagging further under Sigi's weight and it had started to veer southwards from its handlebar attachment. Soon it was going to hit the wheel guard. After all I had bought it very cheaply and it was only ever designed for shopping. After a quick search I found a German company called Rixen & Kaul who made sturdy-looking carriers. As I was being careful not to overspend, I ordered up a basic design. It would keep us going for a while and when it arrived Sigi took to it straight away.

Each week my videos were becoming more adventurous. I was still using the free software that I'd found online but now I was perfecting the art of editing. On some videos I speeded up sections for comic effect or in places where there were dramatic scenarios, like Sigi chasing a squirrel, I slowed down the footage. Funnily enough, I'd never seen myself as a creative person at all – always the data science guy – but I was enjoying discovering this new and unexpected side to myself. Without sounding too grand, I stopped seeing the videos of me and Sigi as clips and more like snippets of art, as if I was making a body of work not unlike a tattoo or graffiti artist. Instead of the human body or walls as my canvas, social media was my medium. Since I'd attached the selfie stick my videos were also looking far more polished by comparison and getting hundreds more views. But why some clips attracted more attention than others, I had no idea. It all seemed very random.

One video I posted up was a compilation of several trips out that we'd completed over the past six months. It attracted nearly forty thousand views. I found it hard to believe. Why had that

video in particular been so popular? When I thought back to
the online bingo game that I'd created in Silicon Valley, I tried to
reason it out. By adding a range of special features, it had gone
from an average-selling game to a bestselling game. But in that
scenario there was the possibility that people could win prizes
and money. Online gambling elicits a bonkers dopamine hit,
similar to other online games where there are rewards or points
to win along the way. But by watching Sigi no one actually won
anything, except maybe a tiny moment of joy. It made me want
to play around and investigate further.

So far, Instagram had been the main platform where I
posted videos of Sigi. Previously I'd uploaded a small amount
to YouTube featuring longer-format adventures, but these
were nothing creative. Rather those were just the raw footage
of videos I edited down for Instagram. As for TikTok, I knew
about it but I'd never joined it, that is until I met Zombie
Punk.

Camden Town was becoming a regular destination for us,
especially the market area where people flocked to say hi to Sigi.
Almost every day I'd seen a heavily tattooed guy sitting on the
bridge that stretched over the canal. He held up a sign which
said: HELP A PUNK GET DRUNK. If anyone wanted their
photo taken with him, he charged £1. The sign always made
me laugh. On occasions I'd seen small crowds gathered around
him. Tourists, I guessed. A punk with a black and bright-pink
mohican, leathers, tartan trousers and chains was pretty hard
to ignore. Occasionally he smiled at Sigi if we rode past, but I'd
never actually stopped to say hi.

In early summer, curiosity got the better of me. As we approached I hopped off my bike and took Sigi over. 'Hey man, how are you?' I said.

'Hi,' he smiled. Immediately I could see he didn't have a whole lot of interest in me. Instead, he made a beeline for Sigi. 'What's her name?' he asked, giving the top of her head a gentle pat.

'It's Sigrid,' I replied.

'Sigrid', he repeated. 'She's so calm,' he continued. I could hear from his accent he wasn't British.

'Where are you from?' I asked. When he looked up I could see it wasn't just his hands or his face that were covered in tattoos. One of his eyeballs had been inked completely black. I couldn't stop staring at it. It looked both bizarre and amazing.

'Brazil,' he replied.

We hung out with him for a while. I'd been to Brazil many years ago when I was living in the States, and loved it, so we chatted about the country and why he was in London. His real name was Anderson, he told me, and he was in the UK as a political refugee. He'd spoken out against the Brazilian government and couldn't stay in the country of his birth.

'You're filming everything?' he asked.

'Yeah, I make videos and post them online,' I explained.

'I'm on TikTok. I have loads of followers. You should post there,' he said.

'Thanks. I'll give it a go.'

We said our goodbyes but not before I took Sigi from the carrier and let him hold her. She clambered into his arms and stayed there for a while until she got restless. When we arrived home, as well as editing my video for Instagram, I set up a TikTok account and posted an identical clip there.

'Hey, we made a new friend today, Sig,' I said, showing it to her.

As it turned out we didn't just make one new friend. A few days later when I checked the account I'd amassed 5,000 followers on TikTok. When I first saw it I thought I'd misread it, but the number was there in black and white. It was mind-blowing. Loads of people who'd seen the video had tagged me into the page of Zombie Punk, which is where I first learned Anderson's punk name. From then on whenever we stopped by to see him, I made sure to include the hashtags #zombie and #punk in my posts.

That week another message landed in my Instagram feed. It was from the company Rixen & Kaul, who I'd ordered Sigi's new basket from. *We noticed you were using one of our baskets. Did you know we design a basket especially for pets?*

Admittedly, I didn't, I didn't even know pet baskets existed. The post asked me to private-message the company, which I did.

Would you like us to send you one? a further message read. The basket they were offering me had been designed for dogs but a cat would fit fine.

Sure, I replied immediately. Within days Sigi's new basket had arrived. By comparison, it was the height of luxury, complete with a cushion at the bottom, a built-in leash and a rain cover. It looked incredibly slick and also solved another problem. I'd never had a rain cover before. While I never cared much about the wet, I never wanted Sigi to endure it, knowing how she hated rain. Now we could explore in all weathers.

While the basket was very welcome, the flurry of messages did prompt me to reflect again. Before then, I hadn't been thinking about my videos in that way at all: becoming the recipient of free stuff was not the reason why I had started posting. Instead I'd seen it as an opportunity to share the happiness that cruising around with Sigi gave me and to reach out to a bunch of like-minded people. If I'm being truthful, I also loved showing Sigi off. She's beautiful. I didn't know too much about being a social media influencer, but I did understand that lots of people who got rich online did so because they agreed to advertise anything and everything or be sponsored by any company, regardless of whether it chimed with them or not.

Back in San Francisco a friend of mine was a bona fide social media influencer. She ran a series of online make-up tutorials and received a mountain of free kit from companies to promote. *Did accepting a basket make me an influencer?* I asked myself. I was a guy who preferred to pursue an opportunity without any given goal. Besides, if I was going to promote anything for any company I reckoned it 100 per cent needed to have relevance to Sigi. When I chewed it over, being a brand magnet just didn't appeal. Not long after, when a company did approach me and offered me free cycling fitness classes, I turned them down. Videos of me spinning on an indoor bike would promote the brand but when I asked if Sigi could join in the answer was no. After numerous messages from jewellery companies too, it only confirmed to me that this was advertising money I didn't want to take. Sigi was a cool cat for sure, but I wasn't going to dress her up in bling like a feline Kim Kardashian. *Nice to be asked,* I thought, *but no thanks.* Of course, my precarious financial situation may mean in the future I would have to compromise, but for now I made a pledge to avoid the temptation. I wanted to stay true to myself.

One offer that did come my way that got me excited was from the UCI, which is the Union Cycliste Internationale. When I first looked at the communication from a guy called Zack I was speechless. The organization is based in Switzerland and it's the world governing body for sports cycling. In my wildest dreams, I'd imagined myself as King of the Mountains in the Tour de France, zigzagging my way through the Pyrenees or the Alps, pitting myself against the best of the best, though realistically I'd made do with watching the TV highlights. Zack was the digital content manager at the UCI and he wanted to use some of my existing Instagram clips to promote World Bicycle Day. He also asked if I would record an additional promotional video. The UCI couldn't pay me for the content, but it was a chance to reach out to cycling enthusiasts across the globe. World Bicycle Day? I'd honestly never heard of it.

Apparently the day had been on the annual calendar since 2018, declared by the United Nations General Assembly to promote the bicycle as a simple, affordable and environmentally friendly way of getting from A to B. When I read its Wikipedia entry it also said it had been established to promote the bicycle as a symbol of social inclusion and peace – an emblem of human progress. I smiled. If ever something in my life had brought me a more peaceful way of being it had been cycling with Sigi. A perfect fit, I figured.

But how the hell did Zack find me? I asked. In fact, I'd reached him via one particular video. When I'd made the clip only weeks before I'd been testing out a second pair of goggles on Sigi. After seeing Gary, the first pair I'd ordered up were too big and had sat clumsily across the bridge of her nose. She shook her head frustratedly and attempted to paw them off. This pair were smaller with purple rims and clear Perspex lenses.

'Here Sig, to save you from the wind,' I told her, bringing the strap across the back of her head and fastening the buckle at the back. They fitted perfectly.

On that ride out she didn't shake her head once. Even facing the wind's direction she didn't look back, keeping her eyes firmly on the road. What it was about that video I have no idea, but not long after I'd uploaded it I noticed the viewing figures skyrocket. Whereas the most popular of my clips had been getting 10,000 views tops on Instagram, this started climbing to well over 70,000. At the time, I was mostly intrigued. With hindsight I'd say it was the first of our clips that ever went viral. Through people sharing it over and over it had spread out way beyond my own group of followers and that had included Zack.

As well as using that clip, Zack wanted the additional video to be of me speaking. On the morning we were to shoot it, Sigi and I headed to Primrose Hill. At first, the words Zack wanted me to say seemed a bit nonsensical. All I had to do was look directly into my GoPro and say: 'And don't forget this.' I positioned the selfie stick head-on and recorded several versions. By now I'd got used to being on camera, but only ever as a sideshow to Sigi. I felt a flutter of nerves and tried to get through it as quickly as possible. Later that afternoon I sent the best cuts over.

I could not have imagined how amazing the finished product would be.

A week later Zack had linked me into the final film. Sigi and I watched together in the study. Mine and Sigi's clip formed part of a montage of all the amazing tricks people could do on a bike, from road racing to mountain biking, BMX stunts to Olympic track cycling to a bunch of kids just enjoying being on their bikes, all with the message: Happy World Bicycle Day. A few days after that Zack sent me another link. The UCI had taken just the clip of Sigi and I cycling and used it for a shorter film on Instagram with my handle tagged. Hilariously, the background track they'd added was 'Ridin'' by the hip-hop artist Chamillionaire, all about being chased by the cops: They see me rollin' / They hatin' / Patrollin' and tryna catch me ridin' dirty'. I erupted with laughter. At times like that I regretted that Sigi was deaf. She definitely would have seen the funny side.

By now I was getting the hang of followers. My page usually got a substantial boost if someone tagged me into their posts. With around one million people following the UCI I had a funny feeling that my account was about to balloon in numbers as a result, but even I could not have predicted the upsurge. That video turned out to be the first really big break Sigi and I got online and it added several thousand to my followers. It felt insane. More and more messages also started popping up, some of which struck a chord: *Your cat's living a better life than me*, read one. *Sigi's living a better life than all of us*, I thought. Others had spotted Sigi's bright blue eyes and some in the know asked whether or not she was deaf.

For the first time, however, not all of my feed was positive. Some people had started to follow me with the sole purpose of reporting me. They said what I was doing was cruel and that I was endangering Sigi by taking her out on the road. The accusations stung hard and I kicked around whether or not to reply. Part of me wanted the argument, but mainly I let it be. In my heart I knew that if Sigi didn't enjoy being my cycling buddy, I wouldn't take her. I also knew that I never took unnecessary risks on the road. *People can think what they like. I know my cat and that what I'm doing is okay,* I reassured myself. It still happens today – occasionally someone tags me into a post to Cats Protection or the RSPCA, both animal welfare charities in the UK. Either that or people accuse me of using my cat for clicks and that Sigi actually hates cycling. Usually I post back a video of her miaowing by the door or begging by her basket in the study.

Because of my posts and my online searches, a lot more cat-related material was also coming through my feed. That had the added bonus of firing my imagination about where to take Sigi. In mid-July, I happened to be at home glued to a livestream video on Facebook of James Bowen. James had been homeless in London, busking and battling addiction, when famously a stray ginger tom, Bob, befriended him and helped him get his life back on track. Bob and James became a sensation after James's story ended up being made into a book and a film called *A Street Cat Named Bob*. Tragically Bob died in a car accident in 2020, 13 years after James adopted him. James and his followers worldwide had spent two years raising money to erect a memorial bench and statue of Bob in Islington, the area where James ate his lunch most days and Bob was well loved. The livestream was the unveiling of the statue created by an artist called Tanya Russell, renowned for her bronze animal sculptures.

As I continued watching, I had the sudden urge to take Sigi and join the small crowd of well-wishers. James wasn't someone I knew, but his special friendship with Bob resonated deeply with me. As his speech got under way, it was clear what an emotional occasion it was for him. I glanced over at Sigi curled up next to my keyboard. The idea of not having her in my life overwhelmed me and I also felt a lump in my throat. Losing a cat like that would be devastating for anyone. James should have his quiet moment of remembrance before Sigi and I put in an appearance.

As it turned out, by the time we arrived half an hour later James had disappeared. Understandably Bob's statue unveiling had unsettled him and he needed time to collect himself, but Sigi ended up being her usual calming force among those still hanging around Islington Green. Sure enough, we couldn't have met a more dedicated group of animal lovers who were so gentle and warm towards Sigi. She was curious about Bob too. The minute I let her hop up on to the bench her affection for him was instantaneous. She sniffed around his bronze scarf before stretching up on her hind legs and planting a kiss right on his face. *Maybe she thinks he's a real cat?* I questioned. Whichever way it was super-cute and Bob's and James's supporters felt the same. When I turned around there was a wall of cameras capturing the moment when Sigi paid her own special tribute to a feline icon.

As well as seeking out places to take Sigi myself, followers were also now contacting me with suggestions and also people to meet. One of those was a woman called Rachel. I'd first bumped into Rachel at the back of King's Cross Station in a swanky new area of restaurants and shops called Coal Drops Yard. She'd come over to say hi to Sigi and had followed us ever since. Rachel played with the Royal Philharmonic Orchestra.

Hey, I'm in North London. I'm recording a film score in Abbey Road Studios. Why don't you come down with Sigi? she encouraged me, knowing I lived not far away. It didn't take a whole lot of persuasion. Abbey Road had been on my list of places of interest, being the studios where the Beatles recorded their 1969 album of the same name. Not that I am a huge Beatles fan, but I had considered recreating the album cover of the Fab Four walking across that iconic zebra crossing outside. I'd wanted to use Sigi as the Beatles' substitute but hadn't yet worked out a way to film it.

You won't be able to come inside, Rachel warned, but she asked me to message her when we arrived so that members of the orchestra could step outside on their break. *Seriously? An orchestra wants to meet us?* It didn't seem real. But as soon as we rocked up Sigi was in her element. I let her out on the leash to stroll past the studio wall painted with a mural of George Harrison and plastered in graffiti signatures. One by one a small group of musicians trickled out of the building headed by Rachel.

'Oh Sigi, you came!' Rachel beamed as she bent over to land a kiss on Sigi's forehead. 'Come inside. I can only take you so far.'

She beckoned us into the car park, probably sensing mine and Sigi's curiosity. Members of the public were strictly prohibited beyond the studio's main gate, but Rachel could take us as far as the front steps for a sneaky peek in.

'What are you recording?' I asked.

'Oh we're with Hans Zimmer,' she said casually.

'Hans Zimmer?' I gulped. *The* Hans Zimmer? The famous film composer who'd penned scores for blockbusters like *Thelma & Louise* and *Driving Miss Daisy*, plus a whole load of sci-fi classics like *Blade Runner*? Wow.

As we approached I could feel Sigi pull harder on the leash. 'Hey Sig, you can't go in!' I called ahead, but there was no stopping her. 'Oh sorry,' I apologized to Rachel as Sigi broke through the threshold and sauntered up the stone steps.

Rachel giggled nervously.

'Oh I knew this would happen,' I said embarrassed. What I didn't mention to Rachel was that secretly I wanted to see how far Sigi would get. After all, *the* Hans Zimmer was inside.

'It's cool,' Rachel reassured me. Security guards would eventually turn her back, she explained, but Sigi kept on climbing. One musician lugging a cello edged passed her just as she reached the door.

Then from inside I heard a chorus of voices. *Gonna get thrown out any minute*, I thought. But no. When Rachel and I stepped inside two security guards had dropped to their knees and were all over Sigi.

'Oh my God she is so cute!' they were shouting.

Eventually when one looked at me with the GoPro he wagged

his finger. I readied myself for being removed, but he leaned in and whispered, 'You can't film in here or post anything, but come in,' he instructed. It was obvious they couldn't resist Sigi.

'Hans Zimmer is literally in the next room.' Rachel pointed to a set of double doors.

He could come waltzing down the corridor any minute, I thought. 'She's my access-all-areas cat,' I joked.

That day sadly we didn't get to meet Hans Zimmer but the security guards did let Sigi into their booth where she became mesmerized by the CCTV screens and got to chew on a couple of plants.

'Thanks so much for bringing her,' they both said as we left.

'Mission well and truly accomplished!' I joked to Sigi on the way home. I thanked Rachel online later that evening. It had made our day.

The next morning another message from another follower popped into my inbox. *Have you seen Sigi's picture?* the person had messaged.

Where? I replied.

You're in the Big Issue magazine.

Weird. No one had ever interviewed us or contacted us from there, but apparently the photograph of Sigi kissing Bob the cat had made it to that week's inside page. James Bowen had been a regular seller of the *Big Issue,* the street magazine which is sold by homeless people and helps them get back on their feet financially. It had covered the unveiling of the statue in Islington Green. I rushed down to the supermarket on England's Lane where one woman had a regular pitch and bought a couple of copies. Sure enough Sigi was there in glorious technicolour beside an article about James and Bob. A warm glow crept through me.

'You're the luckiest cat in the world,' I smiled at Sigi. My followers had been right. Sigi was living a better life than all of us.

12

PARTY ANIMAL

'Hey you!' I'd heard the yell from behind, but daren't take my eyes off the road. Sigi and I were just north of Hyde Park on a busy street called Sussex Gardens when the cry was followed by the screech of tyres. Mat had been right when he'd warned me all those months ago: when Sigi and I were cycling during lockdown, we'd experienced the city in the lap of luxury. The volume of traffic was zero compared to late summer 2021. Now we were having to negotiate London's wild nose-to-bumper queues for real.

'Hey, what the fuck?' I heard the cry again, this time with added expletives. *Don't turn around*, I thought. Clearly a guy who hates cyclists. *Ignore him.* Out of the corner of my eye I saw a white van pulling up at the traffic lights where we'd come to a halt. Eventually when I did glance over the driver was leaning from his window, his face crumpled up like a British bulldog.

'Why the fuck are you filming me?' he growled. Sweat trickled down his forehead as he worked himself up into a lather.

So far, I'd experienced zero abuse for cycling with a selfie stick and a camera, but I knew from other cyclists how drivers hated cyclists filming.

This guy clearly thought I was recording him. He revved his engine hard.

'Calm down, man,' I said, feeling pretty pissed off. I leaned back to reveal Sigi, who was hanging over the basket giving him a contemptuous look. 'Can't you see I'm filming my cat?' As the words dropped from my mouth, I did realize how odd they sounded.

But it turned out to be another day for firsts. Immediately, his eyes softened and a warm expression broke on his face, like he'd been struck by Cupid's arrow. I'd only seen something vaguely similar at the anti-vax protest, but this was a dramatic U-turn. 'Hey kitty! Who's a gorgeous cat, eh?' He wiped the sweat from his face and stretched out his hand, making sucking noises with his teeth. 'Here kitty!' he continued. Sigi hesitated before she leaned in and gave his podgy fingers a forgiving nuzzle. 'Sorry mate', he said guiltily. 'Thought you were recording my number plate. Hadn't seen your cat.'

'It's okay,' I replied. I'd been ready to snarl back and probably report him, but I should have known that Sigi would sprinkle her magic dust over the situation. She definitely had the feminine touch.

Others had started recognizing that too. Around the same time a woman called Esra had got in touch. She was from a movement called Fancy Women. I'd never come across it before but she asked if Sigi and I would be interested in heading its

annual bike ride through London. Fancy women? I assumed
these were women who loved to dress up. *Maybe another thanks
but no thanks offer,* I thought. Yet when I read up about it, I felt
very flattered. The bike ride was mainly for women and the
event was started in the port city of Izmir in Turkey in 2013
by a teacher called Sema Gür. Initially it was to spread the idea
of car-free cites, but over the years it has come to represent
freedom for women and especially freedom of movement, which
is restricted for many women living under oppressive regimes.
I'd also previously read about how the bicycle was a key part of
women getting the vote in the UK in the early 20th century,
when suffragettes travelled by bike displaying VOTES FOR
WOMEN banners. It had a lovely quiet campaigning air about
it. Of course, I wasn't naive enough to think it was me Esra was
interested in. She only had eyes for Sigi.

'Your cat's a girl, right? We'd love to have her,' she said.

'We'd love to come!' I replied. The ride was a month away
so I made a note to pick out an outfit for Sigi that reflected the
enormity of the honour.

Meanwhile, information on other cycling-focused protests
were landing in my feed that also pricked my interest. In
particular, the London Cycling Campaign were staging a
protest in central London. One particular gyratory there is
super-dangerous and it has become a notorious black spot for
cyclists, claiming several deaths over the past decade. I recalled
that anyone who had cycled into work had complained that there
was no physical separation between the traffic and cyclists at its
busy intersection and no safety measures in place. If Sigi and

I could help highlight how important cycle safety is then it was an event worth attending and sharing.

Sure enough, being back in the City felt weird. I hadn't visited that area since the previous year when I'd met with Brandon and was put on furlough. In truth, I'd actively avoided it. Whether out of embarrassment or shame I hadn't wanted to run into anyone. I'd not really kept in touch with work colleagues, although a couple had reached out. In those early days redundancy had felt too raw. Now, I imagined a scenario where I'd randomly meet someone who would ask what I was doing. What would I say? I'm still out of work, living as an illegal immigrant and cycling with my cat. All of my better instincts knew that would be judged as an epic fail by anyone who didn't truly know me.

The protest began at around 5.30pm, bang on rush hour, and had been organized in the wake of the death of another cyclist. A paediatric doctor, Dr Marta Krawiec, had been hit by a lorry turning and had tragically lost her life. By the time Sigi and I arrived several hundred people had gathered at the Barbican meeting point – a sprawling complex of arts venues in East London built in the Brutalist style of the 1960s. The mood on the day was one of peaceful protest rather than sombre. Everybody wanted to make some noise and the turnout was impressive. Despite it happening because of awful circumstances, I felt inspired by the show of support but also the campaign's determination. It wasn't only highlighting this junction. Members had also been pushing the London mayor and the city's transport authorities to look at 21 more junctions across the capital that it had identified as dangerous. In my view, any death on the road was one death too many.

'Hey, long time no see!' No sooner had I parked up my bike when I recognized a voice. My fixed-gear buddy Olivier was hovering by my shoulder stroking Sigi. I couldn't help smiling when I realized he wasn't talking to me.

'Hey man, good to see you,' I said. It was great to bump into Olivier again, this time with his girlfriend Nadine, and completely by accident too. He had been following mine and Sigi's travels on Instagram, he told me.

We chatted for a while before the ride got under way. However, as we made our way through Holborn I became more nervous. Now, cyclists were stopping me every few metres, sometimes switching to hands-free while they rummaged in their pockets to find their mobile phones to take a snap. One guy was so taken with Sigi that he almost veered into the side of us.

'I've seen you on Instagram!' another shouted out as he rode past.

'Oh, right on,' I replied. I was trying to take it all in my stride. It felt exhilarating but also kind of scary to meet so many people following me online.

Then, from the corner of my eye I spotted a woman perched cross-legged on the front of a cargo bike with a telephoto lens pointing in our direction. Unsure it was for us, I leaned back so that she could get a better view of the peloton.

'No it's you I want! Carry on as you are,' she called over.

I pulled an embarrassed face, feeling slightly baffled as she clicked away. At the end of the hour-long ride she came over and introduced herself.

'I'm Honor. Honor Elliott,' she said, staring adoringly at Sigi.

'Are you a photographer?' I asked.

Apparently Honor had been a track cyclist, but had got ill and was now pursuing her passion for photography. As well as taking photographs of cycling events she also had a personal project on the go documenting cyclists who rode with their pets, although her portfolio mainly featured dogs. She lived on a houseboat in London, she explained.

'Great to meet you,' I smiled, as Sigi and I turned to leave.

'Here. Take my details. Maybe you and Sigrid can come for a professional shoot one day?' she said.

'That would be awesome!'

Everybody at the London Cycling Campaign had been very welcoming and when I uploaded my footage the next day, I felt genuinely happy to be part of their cause. I'd not ridden before with such a fun and friendly bunch.

That week, I also had time to try out a few new tricks. The more content I uploaded, the more frustrated I'd become with the basic editing software I'd been using. After a little research I found another more sophisticated free package called DaVinci Resolve. It would allow me to experiment with subtitles and a variety of effects. I had another motive too. *USA Today,* one of the US's bestselling newspapers, had contacted me. It had seen my footage and wanted to feature some on its online site. Again, I was blown away. Since running the analytics on my Instagram I knew that I had followers in the States, but a major national newspaper? They weren't offering to pay me but I really didn't care. I was just thrilled that Sigi and I would be seen on our home turf. I sent the editor some clips from which they built a bite-sized digital story. In the UK the *Independent* newspaper also wanted to do the same. This time I'd been approached through a news agency and was offered a small fee. Whether I was being paid or not, with more interest in Sigi I wanted my footage to look even more polished.

One of those experiments was to livestream one journey. Although I'd followed many livestreams online, I'd never hosted one myself. The only drawback was that I wouldn't be able to film it using my selfie stick. Everyone chats online during a livestream event and so I strapped up my phone to the handlebars so I could follow the conversation. I only hoped followers wouldn't be too disappointed with a view of the back of Sigi's head.

On that particular morning the weather was glorious and Sigi and I ventured out to Primrose Hill. In all the time I'd been in London, I never tired of its panoramic views. I'd also taken the opportunity to test out one of the bike rentals that run across London. During the pandemic more pay-as-you-ride schemes had sprung up across the city and had become a welcome alternative for commuters who didn't want to be crammed like sardines on public transport. But the minute we got to Primrose Hill, it hit me that this would be a tense affair. In the months that we'd been riding together Sigi had developed a real hatred for dogs. Where it came from, I have no idea. Back home in San Francisco one of our friends owned a gorgeous husky called Kaiyuh, who Sigi adored. Whenever we hung out together in Golden Gate Park she'd sit beside him and even curl up against his feet in the afternoon sun. But since hitting the UK, dogs had become strictly off the menu. Whenever she saw one, she raised herself up like a king cobra, launched forward, revealed her fangs and hissed pure venom in its direction. At first I felt sorry for Sigi, but as time had gone on it was the dogs I pitied the most. Sigi is seriously menacing when she's angry.

That day I'd planned to pick up some sandwiches and hang out with a picnic but when we got to the park it was obvious everyone else had had the same idea – only the world and its dog had brought along their canine buddies. Sigi couldn't sit still without hissing at one or another, some of whom had innocently bounded over just to say hi. 'Sorry! She hates dogs,' I found myself apologizing to owners.

I was starting to get tired of the sound of my own voice. Maybe it would be less busy on Hampstead Heath, but after a quick cycle there I realized that wherever we went that day, Sigi's four-legged nemeses were out in force. 'Okay, no stopping for us,' I told Sigi, hoping that the ride would distract her.

The rental bike wasn't quite as smooth as my own. Moreover, the cycle paths were gravelly and bumpy but that did have the added benefit of extra vibration for Sigi. And the livestream turned out to be a ton of fun. I managed to pull in around a hundred people all asking about and commenting on Sigi. Some viewers were alone working from home in different parts of the world and had reached out to say that Sigi and I were keeping them company. Having worked in the same way from San Francisco for a whole year, I empathized immediately.

In the end, we did stop briefly for a rest on a bridge above the River Fleet – a tranquil stretch of water that used to run through the city, but is now London's largest subterranean river. One of the only locations to see it above ground is on Hampstead Heath.

'Is she a Norwegian Forest cat?' A voice interrupted us as we stood gazing down at the lily pads and the ducks sailing down the river. A woman had been strolling with her husband and had come to give Sigi a tickle.

'You guessed right,' I said. It turned out she was an owner – the first I'd met since being in London. She had two Forest cats – Morten and Mags – hilariously named after a couple of members of the 1980s Norwegian band A-ha. We compared notes for as long as Sigi could hold out, but the onslaught of dogs got too much and soon it was time to push on. 'Oh dear, gotta go,' I said.

It was now only a few days until the Fancy Women bike ride and I laid out Sigi's ensemble: a Barbie-pink dress with a net tutu. I'd always loved it, but I was unsure she would feel the same. I'd bought it for her back in San Francisco for her first birthday party. We'd never been quite sure what date Sigi was born so we'd jokingly celebrated on April Fool's Day. Now, though, it might not be the feminist statement Sigi wanted to make, but I'd chosen it for the Fancy Women ride to match the pink tie and waistcoat I'd have on for the occasion. As probably one of a handful of men there I wanted to look presentable. Besides, we were leading with Esra – other men were only allowed at the rear of the peloton. Sigi would never have forgiven me if I let the sisterhood down.

'Like it Sig?' I said, fastening it round her and pulling up the mirror. She stared quizzically at her reflection before wandering over to my bike and miaowing. I took that as a thumbs-up.

Bianca joined us that day. She'd been riding out with us more and gaining confidence on her bike and in the busy traffic. As we approached the meeting point in Trafalgar Square loud music blared from a sound system strapped to the back of a trike bike. Sigi leaned in to the rhythm, hanging her paw off the basket like a hip-hop queen. I was anxious we might be overdressed, but it turned out we'd pitched it just right. Women were out in force head to toe in pinks and polka dots with flowers and balloons decorating their bikes. The vibe felt so positive.

'You must be Sigi . . . and Travis?' Esra found us in the square and came over to say hi. 'I hoped you'd make it. Thanks for coming,' she continued.

'Wouldn't have missed it for the world.'

'Could I?' She pointed at Sigi. Not happy with stroking Sigi, Esra wanted to give her a full-on cuddle.

'Oh sure!' I said, lifting her out of the basket and passing her over. Sigi snuggled in looking like she was loving the attention.

The ride took in all of the city centre. First we weaved down The Mall and then up and around to hit Oxford Circus before the peloton looped down to Piccadilly Circus. Onlookers lined the route and many waved and pointed as Sigi and I drifted past.

No sooner had we landed back in Trafalgar Square than I felt a tap on my shoulder. The owner of the trike bike loaded with speakers had headed over. During the whole ride he'd been pumping out disco grooves. 'Hey, I'm Sol,' he smiled.

'Hey, good to meet you. Good tunes,' I replied.

'Yeah, loved doing the music for this ride. You ride fixed-gear?' he said, scanning my bike.

'Yeah, you?'

'Sure!'

When he wasn't DJ'ing for Fancy Women, Solomon also dabbled at being a musician and also DJ'd for a fixed-gear group called Fixed Pirates Crew – a loose collective of riders who came together from all over London not unlike the #bikelife movement.

'Would be great to see you and your cat at Dom Whiting's ride. Why don't you come?' he said.

'I'd love to, but . . .' I shrugged. I admitted I had no clue who Dom Whiting was.

'He's a DJ. Been organizing the drum 'n' bass raves,' Sol said enthusiastically.

'Sure, I'll take a look,' I promised.

Dusk was falling and Bianca and I thanked Esra for the afternoon and headed home. When I thought about it I reckoned Sigi would love drum 'n' bass. The beats would have her so blissed out.

'Such a party animal!' I called over as she perched her paws on the basket rim taking in the evening air. Sigi was amassing a busier social calendar than Bianca and I put together.

When I searched online, I was surprised Dom hadn't come through my newsfeed before. He was a DJ who'd not been permitted to work indoors since the pandemic started. Like all of us, he'd gone stir-crazy but had the idea to get out on his bike and take his set to the masses. He'd been leading on-the-road raves all over the country throughout successive lockdowns. Anyone could join for free, get out in the open air and let off some steam. He had thousands of YouTube followers and many of his raves had gone viral.

When I messaged, him tagging him to my page, he responded almost immediately. We talked a little. Dom asked all about Sigi, signing off with: *Back in London soon. Definitely bring your cat!*

Dom Whiting's ride was happening in late September so I marked it on mine and Sigi's calendar. I had no idea what to expect. I'd already encountered some surreal sights in London, but nothing could have prepared us for that day. When we made it into Hyde Park where the ride started it didn't take long to spot Dom. He was the guy with outsized green headphones balanced on his trike bike with the most elaborate mixing desk and turntables attached. A massive speaker system was wired up and sat in a front cargo box. Behind him were hundreds of cyclists queued up and ready to ride. All types of bikes were on display alongside people balancing on electric scooters.

'Want to get up close?' I asked Sigi. Curiosity had got the better of Sigi and she was already up on her hind legs scanning the horizon. As I watched her a feeling of pride filled my chest. That Sigi was so comfortable in the presence of so many people made me feel thankful I'd taken her to those early gatherings. Undeniably the atmosphere felt a little edgy as if months and months of a pandemic were finally lifting and all the pent-up frustration of the past 18 months was about to be unleashed. We took our place at the front and while I wanted to be in the thick of the action, I also chose a spot where Sigi and I could exit if we needed to.

Dom was surrounded by people, but in a quieter moment I wheeled Sigi over and gave him a fist bump. 'Hey man, we came,' I said.

'Oh great to see you. This must be Sigi.' Dom could not have been friendlier. Hovering by his side was a woman with a tripod and camera. Immediately Dom took me aside. 'Hope you don't mind. These guys are here to interview a few people. Would be cool if you were one of them. Just amazing you're here with your cat,' he said.

'No, not at all,' I nodded politely. In truth, I hadn't felt prepared to be interviewed at all but with a few online articles under my belt I thought, *What the hell?* The reporter looked like a rookie who'd apparently been sent from ITV London. The interview would be going out on prime-time evening news. Dom had also lined up a man called Conrad who'd brought his parrot – a green Amazonian called Dave – who he kept on a leash. *As if this day could get any more surreal,* I thought. Conrad turned out to be a drum 'n' bass enthusiast who had turntables at home but, like me, had initially been anxious about bringing his pet out among a crowd. Yet here he was, a year down the line, and he'd been to most of Dom's raves. The parrot loved them, Conrad told the reporter in response to her question.

She then asked me the same question. 'Does your cat actually enjoy this?' She stared at me, obviously unconvinced.

I should have predicted it. I'd already had so many people enquiring online and my answer was always the same. If Sigi hated it, I wouldn't bring her. I love my cat and I'm never cruel to her. It was hard not to feel a little frustrated.

'She loves it. She'll see me getting my bike ready and she'll be whining at the door. She always seems happy.' I smiled before the reporter thanked me and headed off.

The peloton slowly headed out from Hyde Park and down Constitution Hill. *Bizarre but brilliant,* I laughed as we snaked around Buckingham Palace like a giant pulsating jigsaw puzzle. As well as spinning beats Dom was also MC'ing through a large red microphone and pedalling his bike at the same time. I couldn't take my eyes off him. I was in awe at how he coordinated it all. His performance was seamless. Nothing jumped or scratched as he faded each track in and out.

When I looked around I could see Solomon further towards the back with speakers also attached to his trike bike. He was amplifying Dom's livestream so that cyclists at the rear of the peloton could enjoy the full drum 'n' bass hit. We gave each other a wave.

'Not our usual sightseeing trip!' I called down to Sigi as we made for the South Bank and then eastwards to London's financial district. At times around me I could hear cyclists shouting: 'Hey, I follow you on Instagram!' or 'It's the TikTok guy and his cat!' That felt as unreal as the ride itself.

Can a cat have too much fun? I wondered. For the duration Sigi had her paw resting over the edge of the basket, her head bobbing to the beat.

'Oh my God, look at that kitty!' I heard one woman shout. And when I looked around everyone was cycling and dancing and cheering. Far from being an edgy ride, everyone was having a blast, just pleased to be outside and desperate for a good time after ridiculous amounts of time indoors. Sigi and I ended up staying with the peloton for most of the two-hour event until I could see Sigi getting restless and we ducked out.

That evening Bianca, Sigi, Ylva and I all tuned into the evening news. Seeing the man with the parrot, then me on TV was the strangest feeling. Suddenly I felt very self-conscious. I looked nervous, but Sigi couldn't have looked more chilled. As I sat on the sofa turning the day over in my mind, I reflected on how far Sigi and I had come. Only four years ago she'd arrived at our apartment in San Francisco. I was loving life, blissfully unaware of what a roller coaster the next few years would be. Now we were on prime-time news in a different city, in a different country and surrounded by the friendliest of people. Since losing my job, I ran through all the connections I'd made online and by being out and about with Sigi. Sometimes one positive step is all it takes for good things to come to you. Yet I was also acutely aware of how close I'd come to going under. Without Sigi maybe I would never have taken that step.

13

QUEEN OF THE MOUNTAINS

The messages had started appearing in my feed since 9am. It was mid-October and I was clutching a mug of coffee and checking my Instagram. *You made our morning!* one message read; followed by another, *Wow. Saw you on the way to work.* More and more continued to land. At first I was confused. The messages were coming from Russia of all places – not a country where I thought I had many fans. Apparently a video of me and Sigi riding had appeared on a large digital screen in the heart of the Moscow Metro, welcoming commuters as they made their way to work. No one had asked my permission, but honestly I didn't care. Moscow? That felt wild.

Immediately, I sent a WhatsApp to my ex-girlfriend Teresa in San Francisco. Having worked all the way through the pandemic as an infection control nurse, I'd constantly checked in on her and kept her updated with mine and Sigi's travels, mainly to cheer her up. She'd also been the girlfriend I'd been in a relationship with when I'd adopted Ylva so I knew that my cats had a special place in her heart. Sigi's adventures through London always made her smile.

You're never going to believe it! We were shown on the Moscow Metro this morning, I told her.

I knew the message would strike another chord with Teresa. When she and I were together we'd visited Moscow and St Petersburg as part of a larger trip through Europe that had taken in parts of Ukraine, including the abandoned nuclear site at Chernobyl. In that year – 2012 – Ukrainians were staging a pro-democracy language rally in Kyiv, which we witnessed. All the more poignant now when I think about the brutal war being waged against its people. We'd rode together on the Moscow Metro marvelling at its over-the-top baroque architecture.

OMG. That's amazing. You're famous now! Teresa wrote back.

I had no idea that morning, but that was to be the last message I'd ever receive from Teresa. Only a few days later Bianca and I had been on a bus heading into town when a message pinged up on Facebook. One of Teresa's friends, Ryan, tracked me down to tell me that Teresa had passed. I felt numb. Before Teresa and I had started going out she had battled a drug problem but had sought help and stayed clean. After we'd split it had spiralled again but I always had faith that she would recover. Despite her own demons, Teresa was a person who had always looked out for my mental health – she had the emotional intelligence to pick up on all the cues of when I wasn't coping. Most of all she taught me how to be caring in a relationship, something my own background never had. Her loss felt devastating.

Over the next few days, I contacted friends to let them know. Maybe the circumstances surrounding Teresa's death were too difficult for her family, but as far as I knew there was no public funeral for her, no chance for friends to say goodbye. Instead, over the next few weeks I connected with others who, like me, missed her and wanted to share our memories of better times. In among the sadness, thinking about how far I'd come also hit home. Teresa's death floored me for sure and I ached with an overwhelming sadness, but it didn't destabilize me. A couple of years earlier it almost certainly would have. Instead every morning I kept getting up with Sigi and planning our day. In fact, I came to rely on those days more than ever. Being out with Sigi allowed me to work through my grief, to be distracted by the smiles of people who were happy to see us and to let the good times with Teresa dominate my thoughts. I had never been more grateful to have Sigi by my side.

By the end of 2021 Sigi and I had clocked up more than a thousand miles. We were also featuring regularly in news reports. Our story had been picked up by several more outlets including the local newspaper the *Ham & High*, who interviewed me on Hampstead Heath and sent a professional photographer. A couple of days after the article had run Bianca and I had gone to the Steele for a drink and took a copy to show Stephen.

'Way ahead of you, Travis.' He smiled, pointing up behind

the bar. He'd already cut out the clipping and it was hanging by the row of spirits. 'Rubbish at the pub quiz, but Sigi's quite the celebrity now,' he teased me. It was good to know that in all the upheaval of Covid-19 Stephen hadn't lost his sense of humour or his warm, welcoming spirit that had drawn us in when we first arrived in London.

It seemed Sigi wasn't the only new celebrity in the area. A couple of months before we'd bumped into Lexi in The Washington. 'Know who's moved in?' he said tantalizingly.

'Nope. No idea.' I knew he wouldn't be able to hold the news in for long.

'Go on guess,' he said.

'Just tell us,' we laughed.

'Rita Ora and her boyfriend [now husband], the director Taika Waititi. They've moved into the director Tim Burton's old house,' he said, looking relieved to have offloaded the information. Apparently the house sold for upwards of £8 million. I laughed, but the talk of money left me cold. Unless Sigi signed for a blockbuster film soon, I couldn't see my finances lasting more than a few months but I was determined to keep going. One saving grace was that Bianca's visa had progressed. When it did finally go through it felt like one almighty weight had been lifted from our shoulders. My redundancy and the pandemic had left us trapped and with few options. I was cautiously optimistic that while the year ahead would be hard, we'd keep our heads above water. In fact, it turned out to be a crunch moment. Being legally resident again meant I could apply for full-time jobs without the same pressure. Or . . . I could make a go of it with Sigi. In my head, the way forward was clear. Sigi and I had become our own bosses. We didn't have stupid targets to meet. We didn't have to turn up for work and pretend to be coping. We got up every morning and took each day as it came.

As for being any kind of local celebrity, I was undecided. In part Teresa's last words to me: *You're famous now*, had played on my mind. Of course, she'd written it with nothing but affection but it was a label that brought with it mixed blessings. Being stopped in the street so that people could meet Sigi was a pleasure. In particular, I loved it when children wandered over. 'What's her name?' 'Can we stroke her?' 'Her fur is so soft,' they always commented. The sheer joy on their faces was priceless and it always felt a very humbling experience. After a while it also became the reason that I stopped dressing in Lycra cycling gear. So many kids approached us that I figured for any parent or teacher looking on a forty-something dressed head to toe in tight black might seem intimidating, like a weird version of the Child Catcher in *Chitty Chitty Bang Bang*. Instead I'd cycled only in jeans and a T-shirt or a sweater towards the end of that year. It didn't look half as terrifying.

However, being pointed out as the 'Tik Tok guy' did grate on me occasionally. Increasingly I noticed that groups, especially young girls, had started fawning over Sigi like she was an actual celebrity. Around Christmas time we met a few in Covent Garden: 'Oh wow. You're Sigrid the cat!' When they left us they were giggling and shouting: 'We've met a celebrity!' While I appreciated they were teenagers, it helped me understand that I needed to strike a tough balance. On the one hand, Sigi spread so much happiness that I wanted to continue building her profile online and also in the physical world. I'd even got stickers made with the words 'Travis and Sigrid' which I'd attached to my inside bike wheel so that people could recognize us if we were out and about. On the other, I recoiled from being too gimmicky – recognized simply for existing, like a reality TV persona.

Hilariously I'd also started getting an influx of marriage proposals, some accompanied by a fun laughter emoji, but some more serious requests through private messaging. Sometimes women contacted me with a seemingly innocent question about Sigi, but that soon progressed to whether I was interested in going on a date. *But we've never even met. Besides, I'm married!* I thought. A real ego boost for sure and I did often tease Bianca with clips of women looking adoringly at Sigi as if I were a man pushing a newborn baby in a buggy.

More hilarious was that I often sensed Bianca was a little jealous. While she was, and continues to be, supportive of what Sigi and I were doing, she often joked we were joined at the hip, sometimes at the expense of our relationship. 'Hey, it's our night out!' She rolled her eyes ironically if I picked up Sigi ready to take her to the Steele for the pub quiz.

And if we were out and about together Bianca wasn't as comfortable as I was with the attention we attracted, in part because she often found it baffling and because it took us so long to get anywhere. 'Sometimes I want to go out without being stopped by cat lovers!' she complained, but she also understood the real value and positivity Sigi brought to people.

But for all these reasons, I stuck to my guns of limiting

the advertising I accepted and the messages that I shared or promoted through my feeds. I wanted to feature people and brands who I felt had a genuine connection to Sigi and I.

One of the people I was happy to feature was a woman called Juliet Elliott. She contacted me towards the end of 2021 and asked if she could spend an afternoon with Sigi and I. Juliet had been a model in the fashion industry and a professional snowboarder, but she'd also tried her hand at being a bike courier. Now she's a passionate advocate for cycling and runs her own bike blog Bikes 'N' Stuff. The best thing is she's a cat lover, so she was genuinely interested in how Sigi and I started riding together.

'You must be Travis?' she called over excitedly when we met at the Chamomile Café on England's Lane where Sigi and I had become regulars. As ever, Juliet was talking to me but her eyes were firmly fixed on Sigi. 'She's adorable!' she giggled enthusiastically.

We sat chatting for a while over coffee before heading out on a ride.

'How did you ever get her to sit in the basket like that?' she asked me.

'A lot of patience!' I explained. I recounted to Juliet the story of how I'd first started training Sigi in San Francisco: how I slowly eased her into her harness before walking her around the neighbourhood. And how when we came to the UK, we'd continued walking but after I'd been furloughed we started riding together and picked up the pace day by day. Juliet looked gobsmacked. Her cat, Catwoman, was 14 years old and she reckoned she wouldn't get her anywhere near a basket.

'Yeah, you're probably right,' I agreed. I had trained Sigi from a young age, although I do believe you can train a cat when it's older provided you are prepared to put the hours in.

What I liked most about Juliet was that she seemed genuinely thrilled to be out with us. Despite the intermittent rain that afternoon we took in Regent's Park and did a round trip of Central London. Juliet filmed it for her blog. At one point I heard her shout into her microphone: 'I challenge anyone not to feel happy about a cat riding a bicycle.'

Amazing! Someone who needs no persuasion whatsoever, I thought. There was zero weirdness factor for Juliet at all. She simply instinctively understood the healing power of Sigi.

With the new year in full swing I started checking out local cycle initiatives. When the Camden Cargo Bike Network invited me to learn more about what it was doing I was fascinated. The scheme is run by the local council and operates from a location behind King's Cross Station. When Sigi and I arrived a guy called Gerry came to meet us at the gate. 'Beautiful,' he said, smiling down at Sigi before leading us to an echoey hangar lined up with cargo bikes.

The scheme is designed to encourage businesses to change their transport habits, Gerry explained. Delivery companies or anyone needing to ferry goods around could have a bike on loan for around three months to see if they wanted to make the transition.

'How much are the bikes?' I asked Gerry.

'Some are around five thousand pounds,' he replied. 'We give businesses a free trial in the hope that they will see a bike as an investment in the long term, not just for their business but for the environment.'

Sigi was already sold. I could see her resting on her basket edge almost pointing in one bike's direction.

'Would you like to trial one with Sigi?' Gerry asked.

'Absolutely!'

That morning Sigi and I didn't go far, but just as I had predicted Sigi took to it immediately. For starters the three-wheeler had a far larger basket in front. It swamped her and she looked like a mouse in a trash bin, but it didn't take long for her to climb up the side and balance her paws on the edge. The bike was electric so the ride felt smoother, even as we bumped over cobbles. Just in case, I'd lined the basket with one of the puppy training pads. Sigi was usually a pretty well-behaved guest, but I'd never be able to live it down if she peed on a £5,000 bike.

Of course, when the time came to leave, everyone got their phones out to take a picture. A young reporter had also been there from the *Camden New Journal* and she sneaked in a quick interview. When the article appeared a week later I couldn't help feeling a bit embarrassed. The focus of the bike trial had been about promoting the network, not Sigi, yet it was our picture that appeared alongside many of my quotes. *Maybe that wasn't such a bad thing*, I shrugged. If a cute cat could draw in readers then they'd also learn about the scheme.

That day, we also stopped by to say hi to Zombie Punk in Camden. Now we couldn't cycle past the bridge without a quick pit stop, a fist bump and some quality Sigi time.

'Hey, how have things been man?'

'Good. Can't wait for better weather! How's my favourite Kitty?' he said, giving Sigi's neck a ruffle.

'Oh she's doing good. Just been testing out some bikes,' I said.

However short our interactions, I always came away from seeing Zombie Punk with a sense of wonder. He was out in all winds and weather. He was the antithesis to the suited and booted London commuter in a hurry. He always had time for Sigi and I. On the journey home I also reflected on how my own relationship with the world, especially money, had been changing. Back in San Francisco when I'd been earning a fat salary, I spent money like water. Online, I'd think nothing of ordering up an $800 drone. I'd play with it for a while before my new toy sat back in its box, untouched for months on end. *What was that about?* I asked myself. I came to the conclusion that it was to ease my mental pain. Far from being the panacea I'd imagined, working in Silicon Valley had left me desperate for distractions to get through each day. I'd got into the habit of buying fancy gadgets just for the buzz – constantly seeking an outlet from the stress of my day job. Yet discovering the world with Sigi left me feeling a hundred times more fulfilled, richer both physically and mentally and in ways I couldn't always explain. Instead of focusing inwards, being with Sigi had forced me to look outwards to an undiscovered world.

Now Sigi and I had mastered a fair stretch of London, it was time to spread our wings further. From the first time I'd been to

Cambridge I'd fallen in love with it. Now it was time to show Sigi. I doubted Sigi would last the whole 120-kilometre cycle there so I waited for the first days of spring and hopped on the train. At the other end, I had a route mapped out that incorporated cycling trails around the city and surrounding countryside. Fortunately, I'd also found a room above an old pub that accepted pets – not easy to find, but when I messaged The Waterman it confirmed four-legged friends of every variety were very welcome.

No sooner had we cycled out of Cambridge Station than a group of children ran over.

'Oh wow a cat!' one little boy said, his face lighting up.

'Can we stroke her?' another girl asked.

'Sure, so long as you are gentle,' I told them. My worry with groups of children was always that Sigi would get frustrated with so many fingers running through her hair. Occasionally she would hiss, but that day she seemed up for the adulation.

Another woman stopped us as we drifted into the centre of town. 'Oh you're the Instagram cat!' she shouted. It was one thing being recognized in London, I thought, but in Cambridge? That felt so weird. Then things got even stranger. Just as we were cycling through a cobbled street in the shadow of the famous university spires, I heard a cry. 'Sigi? I can't believe it!'

Hurtling towards us was a woman on a bike. I looked closer to see if I recognized her, but I'd never seen her in my life.

'Hi, I'm Roxanne', she said breezily, in what sounded like an Australian accent. 'You must be Sigi . . . and Travis, right?'

'Erm . . . yeah,' I said, feeling a bit overwhelmed. I also had visions of Bianca with her brow furrowed giving me a hard stare.

Roxanne, it turned out, was a thirty-something Aussie who'd been living in the UK for a while. She headed up the Cambridge Cycling Campaign and had been following us online. Just like the London Cycling Campaign, it is an organization that not only promotes the benefits of cycling for well-being but also campaigns to improve Cambridge's cycling infrastructure and safety. As we got talking I explained that I'd been out with the London organization several times that winter. Only a few weeks before, Sigi and I had joined another protest cycle and I was starting to see some familiar faces.

'I've met some really great people,' I told her.

'How long are you in Cambridge?' she asked.

'We're heading back tomorrow evening,' I replied.

'Have you got time to see what we've been doing around here? If you're free tomorrow maybe we could spend some time together?' she offered.

'Sure, what do you think Sigi?' I looked down, but Sigi was already crouched low in her basket eyeing up a passing Jack Russell. 'The dog is going to regret this,' I joked, as Sigi bounded up, leaped forward and hissed loudly: *Don't mess with me, I've had practise in the big city, buddy.*

'So sorry,' I apologized to its owner. I felt like a record on repeat.

After a good night's sleep and a morning coffee in the pub cafe, we set out to meet Roxanne by the River Cam which winds through the city. The morning was clear but a stiff wind picked up as we powered along the cycleway taking in the beautiful old barges parked up like a ribbon on the waterway. The work of the Cambridge Cycling Campaign turned out to be super-impressive. Not only had it campaigned for more cycle parks around the city to encourage people to alter their transport habits, but it had also been instrumental in establishing cycling and walking trails along the greenway routes. One of those was called the Chisholm Trail, named after a local cycling enthusiast and campaigner called Jim Chisholm.

'Jim first thought of this more than twenty years ago,' Roxanne shouted over. After overcoming many hurdles and lots of local opposition, planning permission for the trail was finally granted and it opened in 2021, she explained. As we continued along beside the river we glided across a brand new steel bridge that now connects small villages to open fields on the opposite bank of the River Cam. On one of the very few stretches where bikes come into contact with traffic, a Dutch-style roundabout had been built segregating cyclists from the traffic, the kind you see on the Continent all the time, and the kind I think other cities desperately need too. As we headed back into town I saw Roxanne point excitedly as we slowed up to some traffic lights.

'It's Jim!' she laughed.

Among a small group of cyclists gathered by the side of the road was Jim Chisholm himself, a bearded man with a grandfatherly face.

'A cat in a basket?' he said, smiling over at us.

'This is a very famous cat from Instagram – Sigrid and Travis,' Roxanne introduced us. At that moment I felt very small. Sigi and I could highlight Jim's incredible work, but his vision and his persistence over decades had made it all happen. I had to take my hat off to him.

'Oh not so famous!' I laughed nervously.

What made me feel upbeat was the amount of people I could communicate the work of the Cambridge Cycling Campaign to. My followers had been steadily growing and that month had hit 60,000 on Instagram. On TikTok they were a staggering 175,000. Although I was now meeting lots more people in the flesh who followed me online, I still found it hard to fathom. Whatever superpower Sigi had, she was bossing it.

I came away from Cambridge thinking that so many of the great ideas I'd seen there could be incorporated into parts of London in the places where cycling infrastructure was weak. And over the start of 2022, I'd come to better understand some of the limitations of the city. Since our chance meeting on Hampstead Heath, Mat and I had bumped into each other on a few more occasions and he'd let me know about an alleycat marathon organized by a cycling club called Fixed Beers, of which he was part. What had started as a casual cycle meet and a few beers with friends has grown to regular rides, its very own race team and a series of cool events, from races through London's labyrinth of underground tunnels called Tunnel Rat to another called Tour de Fixed, a mammoth six-stage race to different locations across the capital all competed on separate days and across three months. Riders complete each stage on their own within a two-week window, moving from marker to marker via a route of their choice to make the fastest possible time. In 2022 there were three different prize categories but Sigi and I weren't serious competitors. Instead, from January through to April we completed the six stages of the race in many bizarre and wonderful locations – some with more potholes than the moon and others with cycle routes that simply petered out.

Certainly, I'd been anxious about taking Sigi. Each route took in around ten checkpoints and while I'd set out to log our Strava times as required I wasn't under any illusion that we could compete with the hardcore fixed-gear racers. Like any alleycat race they would be licking through the streets at pace. With Sigi on board, we'd assume a leisurely pace. Our first Tour de Fixed stage started from the city's maritime heartland in Woolwich and carried on to Greenwich where the famous *Cutty Sark* sailing ship is dry-docked before heading towards Central London. It was 57 kilometres door to door – the longest ride Sigi had ever done, yet she held out brilliantly. With enough pit stops for light refreshment and a stretch of her legs, Sigi managed it with zero fuss. Only towards the tail end of the day could I see her wriggling around in the basket and miaowing in my direction.

'Okay Sig, you've done great,' I encouraged her. That long on the road was pretty impressive and it gave me the confidence to keep going.

The second Tour de Fixed stage happened in February and turned out to be even more mileage. Each marker on the route was a closed down or derelict pub across London and its outskirts and took us from Shoreditch in the east all the way to Ilford in Essex and back through the south-east of the city.

From home the round trip was 70 kilometres. The farther out we headed the worse the roads became. Cycle paths were non-existent and the risks drivers took also seemed to worsen. At times I gulped at the close passes cars made, and on several occasions turned off alongside streets – not great for our Strava time, but worth it for Sigi's safety.

By the time we reached our third pub, the Manby Arms in Stratford, I couldn't help thinking this was a road trip tinged with melancholy. The pub had been boarded up for almost a decade, eerily empty and left crumbling on a street corner. Other pubs were the same – sprayed in graffiti, with peeling paint and whitewashed windows. Bianca and I had fallen in love with pubs from the moment we chose Belsize Park as our home. To see so many going to waste felt like the saddest of history lessons, which hit home when we finally made it to Ilford. I'd stopped by one row of shops on its busy main road. The GPS had directed me to where a pub called The Cauliflower once stood. An old man sitting outside an antiques and collectables shop spotted Sigi and I. 'Looking for something?' he asked.

'Yeah, an old pub called The Cauliflower. Do you know it?'

'You're stood next to it,' he said, pointing over to the right. His eyes looked downcast. In its own grounds the shell of a grand three-storey building was just about standing, shuttered up with corrugated iron windows. *In its heyday it would have been magnificent,* I thought.

'Had my very first pint there when I was eighteen,' the man said.

'Really? Shame it's gone,' I told him.

'London's changed so much,' he continued, his eyes glazing over as he began to reminisce. He'd owned his shop for more than 40 years. So many businesses had come and gone through good times, recessions and now a pandemic.

'Yeah, I lost my job,' I confessed to him.

'Sorry to hear that . . . beautiful cat,' he nodded over at Sigi.

'She leads me and I follow,' I joked, before we left him sitting on an antique chair and set off for our next destination – The Victoria pub near Woolwich.

Over that month and during March, Sigi and I completed further Tour de Fixed stages. We cycled up and down the Thames Path along favourite stretches we'd discovered before. We also took in famous road bollards of London that led us in a zigzag route across Central London. That day it rained non-stop but Sigi refused to shelter under her cover. Instead, she wriggled her head out of the side from the get-go, just in case she missed anything. Like the buildings of London, and me, it struck me how Sigi had changed too. When we'd first come to London she'd recoiled at any spattering of rain. Now under the rain cover, her body stayed bone dry but her face throughout resembled that of a drowned rat. She seemed happy.

Another tour of South London took in the killer hills around an area called Crystal Palace, where one of London's three radio and television masts sits, visible on the skyline from every angle. A day out discovering all the filming locations the cult film *Shaun of the Dead* also allowed Sigi and I to enjoy a whirlwind tour through London's suburbs with their mock-Tudor houses, stone driveways and corner pubs, off the beaten track of the standard tourist trail. Races were great at revealing undiscovered parts of the city, I decided, but they didn't leave us any time to stop. And meeting friends and strangers had become such an integral part of our journey.

14

ALLEYCAT

A message that came through Instagram in late March immediately caught my eye. A producer on the *Jeremy Vine* show on Channel 5 had contacted me asking if I would appear on the programme. Admittedly, I'd never watched the early morning chat show, but I knew exactly who the TV and radio personality Jeremy Vine was. As a well-known advocate for cycling, he's often at the centre of many tussles with drivers, all filmed and broadcast over his Twitter account. I had a lot of respect for his efforts to champion cycling. How could I say no? The piece was to go out in early April, only this time it wouldn't be pre-recorded like previous interviews I'd done. It would be live. When we finally caught up by phone, the producer explained that Jeremy would introduce a debate about the benefits and drawbacks of cycling with your pet before he cut to me and Sigi. In theory it sounded like a breeze, but as the days wore on I began to seriously stress out. While the show's producer hadn't been explicit about the questions that I would be asked, he was keen that when I appeared Sigi needed to be in the frame. 'I'll do my best,' I assured him, but inside I was under no illusions: *Sigi is her own woman – she'll do what she wants when she wants,* I thought.

At around 8.30am I logged on. I'd been awake before sunrise having barely slept the night before. Paranoia had got the better of me. Sigi leaping around during the interview, or miaowing, or disappearing altogether kept flashing through my mind. Or even worse, hissing.

'Are you going to be on your best behaviour today? Not going to embarrass me on live TV?' I asked her as I fed her that morning.

She looked up nonchalantly: *I heard you, but no promises.*

Around ten minutes before the broadcast was due to start I settled Sigi on the sofa. So far, so good. She curled up on her cushion as I gave her gentle scratches and her eyelids contentedly closed. Yet my nerves were jangling. As soon as the feed cut to us I felt a weird out-of-body experience. The debate covered familiar ground – a whipped up controversy for TV, the primary question being: should you cycle with your cat? One panellist thought not and that it was cruel. The other loved the idea of Sigi and I roaming around. I sensed Jeremy Vine was in favour too, although he never explicitly said it.

When I was interviewed I reiterated that I never took unnecessary risks. I had a choice, I said. Either I decided not to live, or Sigi and I lived our best lives. As soon as I'd said it, a strange realization hit me. A few years ago I'd barely been existing, now I was telling a daytime TV audience that I was choosing to live my best life. Inside it struck me that I was no longer on life support but instead supporting life. Not every day was great. Depression can bite you when you least expect it, but every day *was* better. As the camera cut back to the studio the thought turned over in my mind.

As the seconds ticked on I prayed that the segment would end soon. When I glanced over at the clock, two minutes had gone by, then four. All the time, a large digital picture of me remained on the screen while the guests argued back and forth. Every time I felt Sigi move, even slightly, I clamped my hand a little tighter over her back, still trying to smile politely into the camera. There was a read-out of comments from viewers and even a live phone-in – a man named Jeremy called in to say how happy he thought Sigi would be cycling around. But an online question from Brian asked why I would put an innocent animal at risk, especially as many cyclists already complained about safety on the road. It was eight of the longest minutes of our broadcast career. When it finally ended and Jeremy moved on to another topic, my body flooded with relief. *Thank God that's over.* The line clicked off, Sigi looked up casually, hopped off the sofa and padded out, turning as if to say: *You owe me one, Dad.* 'Thanks Sig,' I shouted after her.

On the road Sigi was now regularly attracting drive-by admirers. Black cabs stopped so that passengers could stretch out their hands at traffic lights and give her a stroke. One Deliveroo driver with a pizza in a box strapped to the back of his motorbike got a shock when he found Sigi leaning in and trying to prise open the holdall with her nose. 'Don't worry, she's strapped in. She can't get at it,' I shouted over apologetically, but the courier was already whipping out his phone to take a photo and laughing loudly from underneath his helmet.

Mostly I was astounded by which groups of people Sigi attracted. Women and children had always naturally gravitated towards her, but men in uniform also couldn't resist. Burly builders in hard hats and fluorescent jackets all came to say hi, alongside the police. Train guards and London Underground staff also gave Sigi so much love. The only uniformed guard I have never been able to get to break a smile at Sigi are the King's guards with their scarlet tunics. Whenever we passed through Westminster, which we did often, I wondered how they could ever stay so still mounted on horseback outside Horse Guards Parade and keep a straight face.

In June Sigi and I headed out to join the celebrations for Queen Elizabeth II's Platinum Jubilee. On that long bank holiday weekend I had the idea to head to Buckingham Palace and St James's Park to cheer up some of the crowds who had gathered. Some diehard supporters had been camped out on The Mall for days, many of them waiting in particular for the royal family to stand on the palace's famous balcony and wave to the crowds. I would never call myself a royalist, but I was curious about the British royal family with all its pomp and ceremony. What better place to experience that than at a celebration of the Queen's 70 years on the throne. As soon as we rode that morning, I figured out it was going to be a long day. So many people were out and about and in a holiday mood that we were stopped on every street corner by fans. As we got further into town, cafe and shop windows were adorned with Union Jack bunting and when we finally reached Central London flags lined the main streets.

In Trafalgar Square the police were out in force as a motorcade swept past, but Sigi and I couldn't get a good enough view of who was inside the official car. It was impossible to see past the backed-up traffic. Besides, Sigi was being distracted by a camera crew from an Australian TV channel all of whom were aiming their phones at her. 'She's the real queen,' I joked with them.

That afternoon we were stopped by tourists, couples, royal watchers, couriers, police, park attendants and many, many kids. Sigi was proving to be a real crowd-pleaser, but I was becoming a little anxious. 'Think you need some Sigi time,' I said after a couple of hours. By now Sigi was so used to mobile phones being pointed in her direction that I noticed she often turned her head away. But when she got restless and hissed, that became my cue to take her to a quiet corner and let her out on her leash to give her some undisturbed freedom. That afternoon Sigi's squirrel hunting reached an all-time high as she leaped across the grass and attempted to pounce on a grey squirrel in Green Park. 'Nearly got that one,' I called over. Sigi looked disappointed. No matter how fast she runs, squirrels always outsmart her. This one scurried at lightning speed up a tree, refusing to come down while Sigi dug her claws into its trunk, gazing up through its branches and whining loudly.

At the moment we were heading out of the park I noticed more crowds had gathered all waving their Union Jacks. Blue flashing lights streaked past and we caught a glimpse of a large cavalcade of police on motorcycles. 'It's Harry . . . and Meghan,' I could hear people excitedly murmuring. A loud cheer erupted from people further forwards pressed up against the barrier and it rippled back like a Mexican wave to where we were standing. As the car sped past I spotted the couple smiling and waving from the back seat. 'Hey, saw your first Royal,' I turned to Sigi, but she was knee-deep in her own well-wishers all commenting on how beautiful she was. Some were even calling her 'Your Majesty.' *Trust Sigi to steal the show*, I thought.

Similar comments appeared on my Instagram feed for days. Some of my followers were clearly avid royal watchers, some weren't. That didn't matter to me. I'd set out to highlight unique things happening in London, rather than pass judgement.

Not long after, one post of a pro-abortion rally at the American Embassy Sigi and I stumbled across one afternoon attracted an equal measure of support and criticism. The demonstration was being staged following the overturning of the Roe v. Wade decision in the US, which paved the way for individual states to ban abortion if they wanted to. A backwards step, in my view, but not the view of some of Sigi's fans. Maybe not the view of the UK authorities, either. Sigi and I had never been approached and asked to be super-sleuths before, but just as we were standing on the sidelines watching the demonstration, a couple of officers had quietly pulled us aside. At first, I assumed they had a problem with me cycling with Sigi.

'Do you know the names of anyone taking part?' one asked me in a hushed tone. I was very taken aback. The UK is not known as a police state.

'Nope, sorry. Just filming with my cat,' I said, pointing at Sigi who was suspiciously scanning the men in uniform.

It was at times like that I realized how absurd that sounded, but the officers accepted my explanation and directed their questions to others in the crowd. Even if I had known, I wouldn't have turned supergrass. In my view, everyone has the right to peacefully protest without being spied on or arrested.

At around the same time another strange thing happened. On this occasion, I was less conciliatory about the debate I'd sparked online. At the beginning of July Sigi and I headed down to London Pride, the annual festival celebrating the LGBTQ+ community. Back in San Francisco, Bianca and I had always taken part in the event. Bright banners, colourful costumes and lovely, happy people always drew us in and in London there would be more than enough for Sigi to discover too. As the procession moved from Marble Arch to Oxford Street, admirers covered in rainbow flags ran over to pet Sigi. One man in a kaleidoscopic dog mask bounded over to shake her paw. Would Sigi hiss? Thankfully she saved him from that indignity but she couldn't take her eyes off him. I wondered whether she momentarily confused him with a real dog.

As we made our way through Soho, small queues of people waiting to meet Sigi formed. Everyone had seen us on TikTok or Instagram and couldn't believe they had bumped into Sigi for real. In fact, that afternoon I felt sad to leave the carnival atmosphere behind but after a couple of hours I could see Sigi becoming overwhelmed. Later that evening I edited down my footage and uploaded it. So many people enjoying themselves leaped out at me that the next day I planned to show more of the Pride march.

However, the following morning when I brought up my page I noticed something unusual. My followers had dropped in number – by around 2,000. While I never got obsessed with numbers, checking had become a regular habit. This *was* odd. Normally my followers only increased. *Maybe there was a glitch in the system?* I thought. Sadly not. As I sat with my morning coffee scrolling through my comments, the reason became clear. A percentage of my followers were from countries where being gay is illegal; mainly they were from Saudi Arabia. The Arabic messages were impossible to understand, but some of what people had posted in English turned out to be the most hateful I'd ever seen. *I wish I was there so I could blow up the place,* read one. *That place looks disgusting,* read another. As I continued scrolling, I felt my anger rise. Whatever I showed on my feed, I was always up for a healthy amount of debate, but when it came to outright discrimination and cruelty this hit the limit of my tolerance. Clearly followers had left in disgust, but not before letting their feelings be known. Did I care they'd left? I cared more about their attitude and I didn't want that hatred on my feed. While I didn't expect everyone to share my views or my interests, I did expect some basic human decency. Sigi brought together a wide variety of people in the spirit of peace and live and let live. No great loss, I concluded.

My disappointment and anger lingered for several days, but I kept telling myself that I was right to continue posting up highlights from the march. I wasn't going to let anyone intimidate me or dictate what I showed. And the amazing thing about cycling with Sigi is that negative feelings often faded more quickly and got replaced with positive thoughts, which is exactly what happened a few days later.

I was cycling through Regent's Park when I heard a woman's voice that sounded vaguely familiar. Usually, if people know us they call out Sigi's name, but this voice shouted 'Travis!' When I looked up, one of my former colleagues, Harriet, was waving at me and rushing over. She was with a friend who I didn't recognize. Harriet had worked in the customer support team in Holborn and so we'd spoken almost on a daily basis. Whenever there were bugs or glitches in the system she let me know so the tech team could sort it out. My stomach lurched. *The moment I've been dreading, but it had to happen sooner or later,* I thought. I readied myself for her pitying grimace and 20 questions about my redundancy and what I'd been doing since. I smiled half-heartedly. Inside I was squirming.

'Travis! I've seen you on TikTok!' she called out, her voice reaching fever pitch as she lunged in to give me a warm hug. All of a sudden, I felt my shoulders soften.

'Oh, you have?'

'Yes it's amazing!' she laughed. 'And this must be Sigi . . .'

'Oh yeah,' I replied, now hoping Harriet hadn't sensed my hesitancy.

'So, are you filming right now? Are we going to be on TikTok?'

'Yeah,' I smiled. Her companion bent down, grinned into the camera and gave us a big thumbs-up. I couldn't help swelling with pride. I'd been terrified that colleagues might consider me a failure and judge me for the life I was living. Instead, Harriet was congratulating me for doing my own crazy thing and trying to make a success of it. She wouldn't have known it but that day she made me feel very special and, of course, Sigi got loads of attention too.

Part of doing my own crazy thing, however, was making sure I had enough money coming in. So far, I'd been getting the odd piece of advertising and promotional work which had grown steadily, but it was nowhere near enough to live on. While I didn't like the idea of asking my followers for money, in my heart I knew that to keep making our films I had to. In June I put out an appeal for donations on a site called Patreon which helps support creators by encouraging fans to become regular donors. Admittedly, it was one of the most awkward piece-to-camera speeches I had ever recorded – asking anyone for money always feels like begging – but if Sigi and I were to continue I had to face reality. I filmed it on our front doorstep, edited the film down, took a deep breath and uploaded it. Again, the response was almost instantaneous and when I think about it now I know I am lucky to have such a loyal bunch of people watching our films. Whether people signed up for £1 or £50 a month, sponsors trickled in. It was genuinely overwhelming. The total wasn't a liveable salary, but it certainly meant we could carry on for a while.

Followers had also asked me whether I'd ever thought

about Sigi merchandise. Previously, I had considered it as a possible income stream but I wasn't a graphic designer and I also debated whether people would actually buy it. However, the more requests that poured in, the more I figured I should give it a go, albeit with a very limited selection. In my head, the design was obvious. Sigi hissing at dogs had become a recurring motif throughout my films and a bit of a running joke. Followers loved it. Whenever I put together compilations of Sigi hissing in dog-related incidents, I subtitled the word 'hiss' and likes, shares and followers increased. Plus, when Sigi displayed her fangs she looked like a lioness. I chose the most menacing picture of Sigi hissing I could find and created a design online with the word 'Hiss' written underneath. Today, a Sigi-themed sticker, T-shirt, hoodie and mug remain the items for sale in our shop. Again, my followers didn't disappoint. Not only was the initial batch snapped up, but the stranger aspect to it was that soon images were landing in my inbox: pictures of Sigi's face glued to a person's laptop case, or followers sipping from a Sigi-themed mug, or Sigi out and about on someone's T-shirt. At first I didn't know what to say. It felt so surreal. Yet what was also amazing was that now I could see what many of my followers looked like. They weren't just people with anonymous handles commenting in my feed any more. These were people, with lives and stories that they wanted to communicate. The merchandise wasn't going to make me a fortune, but that was okay. Just seeing Sigi's image and connecting to the many smiling faces all over the world gave me a boost.

What also gave me a boost was the reaction of some members

of my family, especially my dad. Although I hadn't seen him in a few years, I did send him links to my Instagram and occasionally kept him updated on which newspapers Sigi and I featured in, especially once outlets such as *USA Today* had started picking up on the story. Given he had always been an animal lover and in older age he'd mellowed, too, making our relationship a little smoother, I figured he'd enjoy seeing what Sigi and I were up to.

'That's awesome, son,' he told me on several occasions, an acceptance that did touch me even though our contact was sporadic.

My half-brother, Greg, on the other hand, had started following Sigi and I religiously on all our platforms and sent a running commentary on how amazing our journey had been so far. *I can't believe it! You've got thousands of followers!* he said, always pointing out clips he liked the most. Although he'd stayed in the Pacific Northwest, he was doing well and had a successful career in real estate which found favour with my dad and his ideas of being capable and a breadwinner. Somehow, though, it reaffirmed to me that I was right to follow my own path. For Sigi and I it had started to feel as though the world was our oyster.

As the summer continued Sigi was in full shedding mode. Having a beautiful long-haired cat makes for great videos and cosy cuddling but during the hot months I had to factor in a good brush before we left the apartment. My fear was always that Sigi would develop a fur ball in her throat after washing herself, as cats often do. If we were on the road and she started choking things could get tricky. It was already difficult enough to manage her love of chewing plants, which occasionally made her wretch. Now I'm convinced there is not a flower stall left in London that Sigi hasn't sniffed or a park where the foliage didn't end up between her teeth. Sigi has always been a cat of contrasts. On the one hand a peace-loving, flower-power hippy, on the other a daredevil speed-freak. The latter was about to be indulged.

In early August Mat got in touch. Immediately I knew Sigi would love our next adventure. So far we'd cycled the stages of the Tour de Fixed at our leisure, but we'd never accompanied riders on an alleycat race proper. The Great Alleycat of London was happening mid-month. Mat would be competing and others would fly in from the US and other parts of the world to take part. *Maybe we could race a couple of checkpoints just for the thrill?* I thought as soon as the message landed.

The race was to begin at Mint Street Park, not far from London Bridge Station on the south side of the city. By the time Sigi and I got there a crowd of around a hundred had gathered – Mat came over to say hi and some friends were also there from the Fixed Pirates Crew. Others I recognized from online. One guy, Krussia, was a well-known fixed-gear rider from the States who I'd often followed. I felt a tingle of excitement when I saw him aiming his phone camera in Sigi's direction. Another guy, Toni Rodriguez, was also revered in the fixed-gear race scene and was attracting a small crowd. Joseph Kendrick, who I was also introduced to, had cycled some wild journeys. A tall, muscular cyclist, he trained as an athlete and had toured more than 16,000 kilometres around the perimeter of Australia. It sounded almost unbelievable. A 24-hour Deliveroo marathon he'd completed also made me smile. While Sigi and I seemed wild at times, there was always someone who pushed the boundaries further.

As an unofficial participant in the race, my plan was to stick behind the Fixed Pirates Crew, most of whom had bike courier knowledge of the city. Each checkpoint was a street name and those who instinctively knew their way around without having to use Google Maps always got there faster. Soon it was time to set off and I could see Sigi raring to go. She'd been petted to death at the start line and I sensed she needed some cycle time.

'Three . . . two . . . one . . . go!' Suddenly everyone rushed on to their bikes. 'Pirates! Pirates!' supporters on the sidelines cheered loudly, as others filmed us with their phones. As we followed the crew into the bright sunshine, the hum of excitement was palpable. Sigi felt it too. Within seconds she was upright in the basket, paws balancing on the edge and her head swaying from left to right. We swerved under tunnels and along main roads, over bridges and through parks. Although my instinct was to race as fast as I could, I hung back, careful not to put Sigi in any danger. Up ahead I could see fast riders breaking away from the pack, clearly in the race for a podium place. In the end Sigi and I managed two checkpoints ending just north of King's Cross Station before I grabbed a refreshing beer with some of the riders and we called it a day. Sigi clearly had a taste for alleycat racing. *Maybe next time she and I could race a little further,* I thought.

Since I'd started amassing followers on my Instagram page I'd never spoken openly about my mental health struggles. In truth, I was hesitant to do so. My experience in full-time work was that however understanding people said they were, depression is still a taboo subject. Revealing an illness that many find inexplicable feels like a colossal step to take, especially for men. In September, however, I found myself in a situation where I was forced to. Over that month I could feel myself slipping under. Since my redundancy I'd continued to take the antidepressants I'd been prescribed and they had more or less kept me on an even keel, but every now and then life seemed to overwhelm me. Sometimes there wasn't anything specific that triggered it, but over weeks I could feel everything become gradually heavier and life become more effort. Yet with Sigi lovers to satisfy that periodically created a tension. Often I got concerned messages from followers if I hadn't posted a film up for a couple of days: *Are you okay? Has anything happened to Sigi?* It was lovely that people were concerned and genuinely seemed to care about the both of us, but sometimes I felt the pressure. This time, I realized I was going to need more than a couple of days off to focus on my well-being. So followers wouldn't worry, I decided to be honest.

Tentatively, I posted a status update hoping that people would understand I needed time out and had to put myself first – something I'd got a little better at recognizing before it became harder to lift myself out from a crisis. *Having the worst time. Be kind to one another. See you in a few days, Okay?* I wrote. Almost within the hour, one of my followers, Andrea, had messaged me. Andrea lived with her partner Tristram on the other side of London but through my feed we'd become buddies, even hooking up now and again for a coffee or a ride. *Is there anything we can do?* she asked. Andrea and Tristram were people I knew I could confide in. From the get-go, they'd seemed kind and we'd hit it off almost instantly. I'd already opened up to Andrea about my depression on the times we'd talked before.

I don't know. Just feeling terrible, I messaged back.

A while later Andrea replied. *Fancy a trip to the seaside?* she asked, suggesting that she book an Airbnb and we all decamp to Brighton for a couple of days. Some quality walking and cycling time, sea air and a fresh perspective may be just what the doctor ordered.

When I thought about the offer I was blown away by how thoughtful it was. My natural instinct was to shut myself off from the world, but I gave myself a good talking-to. If there was anything that Sigi had taught me, it was that acting counter-intuitively brought rewards. Whenever I felt helpless, she had forced me to engage with the world in a more positive way. She had given me a purpose and a focus. Hiding from reality didn't solve much at all, but being with safe people would be good for me, I reasoned.

I would love to. Thank you, I replied. Reassuringly, other online followers were equally as understanding. I'd felt apprehensive about how they might react, but supportive didn't even come close. *Take all the time you need, Travis*, one wrote. Another message read: *It's okay to withdraw and take time for yourself.* Whatever fear I'd been feeling vanished. I knew I could concentrate on my own health without the added weight of expectation.

As it turned out, a seaside break did wonders for my peace of mind. Brighton became a whole new canvas for Sigi and I to explore without the need to post on social media. After taking her to Cambridge, Brighton had been on my to-do list but we hadn't yet found the time. Instead of cycling there, we took the train and as we careered through the Sussex countryside I already started to feel more upbeat. There was something about getting out of the city that felt cleansing. Sigi spent the journey upright with her face pressed to the window watching the yellow cornfields and tiny villages whizz by.

The apartment Andrea had booked sat a couple of blocks back from the seafront. As soon as we arrived, we offloaded our backpacks and wandered down to the promenade. Immediately, Brighton reminded me of some of the Californian towns we'd left behind that dotted the coastline, filled with fairground attractions and areas of fading grandeur. What I hadn't expected was such a lively atmosphere. As we walked through Brighton, the streets were bustling and Sigi's eyes didn't know what to look at first. A little further out it didn't take long to find quieter stretches.

'We're under no pressure to do anything,' Andrea reassured me. In fact, it turned out to be the most low-maintenance two days I'd had in a long time. In the afternoon, we ventured along some of Brighton's cool cycle paths. One took us all the way out beneath the coastline's famous White Cliffs in the direction of cute seaside villages such as Rottingdean. The chalk sea cliff towered above us and Sigi spent a lot of the journey with her head craned upwards watching birds dive in and out of crevices. What struck me also was the powder-blue colour of the sea. That day was crystal clear and the water glinted like gemstones. However, what caught Sigi's attention as we circled back to Brighton was different. In London, Sigi had got used to pigeons, but seagulls scavenging on the beach was a completely new experience.

On the way home, I had tried to take her on to Brighton's only working pier, the Palace Pier (sometimes called the East Pier). An identical West Pier had become derelict and burned down some decades before and its shell is still visible, but the Palace Pier is filled with slot machines and rides – many bright colours for her to enjoy.

Just as we made our way on, a security guard marched towards us. 'Sorry. No animals allowed,' he said firmly.

'Okay Sig, the beach it is,' I said, disappointedly.

To the right were some stone steps leading to the pebble shore and once we found a quiet spot we sat watching the waves roll in for a while. But no sooner had we settled ourselves than the seagulls started flocking, probably hoping we had food. One had Sigi entranced. It bravely landed only a metre away and she hunkered down until she was almost flat and crawled slowly towards it, tiptoeing precariously across the stones. As she got ready to ambush it, it spotted her and took flight out to sea.

'Better luck next time, Sig,' I said, giving her tail a ruffle, but I didn't fancy her chances with Brighton's seagulls. Earlier I'd seen them ducking in bins and plucking chips and leftovers from discarded trays with their sharp yellow beaks. They seemed fearless and more than a match for Sigi.

The sea air and the ride out nicely exhausted us. After a couple of beers and some food we turned in and Sigi curled up purring beside me on the bed. That night, I had a unexpectedly sound sleep. Already the change of scene was doing me the power of good, and I could feel the brain fog lifting.

The next morning we got up early and wandered through Brighton's labyrinth of lanes filled with coffee bars and art galleries and shops selling everything from second-hand furniture to handmade jewellery. In the afternoon Andrea and Tristram left for London but I stayed on. For the rest of the day I planned to cycle further inland and head home later. Some weeks before, the company Berghaus had asked me to test out some of its outdoor gear and promote it on my feed, so this was a good opportunity to take in some of the surrounding countryside and occupy myself with some light work.

Just north of Brighton the South Downs looked tough enough to give me a good stretch out. In particular, a hill called Firle Beacon promised fantastic views across the English Channel before we looped back on a circular route to the station. Heading east from the apartment we wound our way through streets banked on a steep hill lined with cottages and corner pubs in an area called Kemptown. As we climbed further the city faded from view and the landscape opened out to rolling green hills. Unlike the previous day, the weather was overcast and as we inched up the gradient the wind whipped up. Momentarily I stopped to put on Sigi's goggles but a gust almost sent us into a ditch. As if that wasn't bad enough, when we veered off on to a walking trail and through a freshly harvested field we were greeted by a different kind of security guard: cows.

Sigi didn't know what to make of them. I doubted she'd ever

seen a cow before. The herd was a rich auburn colour, beautiful to stumble across but intimidating to manoeuvre around. A couple casually ambled aside making way for us to pass, but one mother and her calf, who she was feeding, stood stubbornly in the way. Sigi sat in the basket and stared her out.

'Hey, what you doing?' I shouted. I didn't want to disturb the calf or frighten the mother but I did want to keep going. The wind was buffeting around us and we needed to reach a sheltered spot. In the end I cycled slowly round giving them a wide berth, cautious not to startle them or attract attention from a bull.

Past the field, it was time to rest and take in the view. Northwards the hills undulated for miles but when I looked back towards Brighton the landscape dramatically swept down to the coast. On the horizon I wondered whether France might be visible but as far as I peered out I couldn't see land. When I looked down, Sigi was nestling in the grass with her eyes closed. How could she take a nap in this wind? Sigi never stopped surprising me. In that moment, I realized how lucky I was. If there was anything the last two years had shown it was that I could take Sigi anywhere and she took everything in her stride. I took the opportunity to make my film for Berghaus and afterwards called it a day. Back to London and back to reality. Thankfully, I felt stronger to face whatever life threw at me.

15

BEAUTIFUL VICTORY

'I was hoping you'd come.' Eilidh, one of the senior organizers from the London Cycling Campaign (LCC) welcomed us as we arrived at its latest protest. 'This is Sigrid and her human Travis,' she introduced us. By now, there were many familiar faces in the group but also a few others I hadn't yet met.

'Hi everyone,' I smiled.

It was early morning rush hour and the protest was unlike any other I'd taken part in. *Ingenious*, I thought. Supporters clothed in fluorescent jackets would create a makeshift cycle lane by forming a barrier between the traffic and the pavement along a busy and dangerous stretch of road in Shoreditch. Others would cycle down it to show how easy it is to provide for cyclists and keep them safe. That day, I'd felt guilty for forcing Sigi out of the apartment at 7am and into the cold fall air, but this was a route we often travelled and where we'd experienced several close passes from drivers. I wanted to highlight the simple solution on my feed. As I chatted, I noticed Sigi snuck in a few extra winks before we set off.

'Morning Sigi and Travis!' I heard several cries as we powered down the temporary lane with my GoPro out in front.

'Hey, great to see you,' I shouted back. A year ago I didn't know what the LCC was. Now I felt like part of the furniture, albeit on two wheels.

'Will you drop by the office some time?' Eilidh asked before we all dispersed. Some activists had office jobs to go to and had come to the protest on their way to work.

'I'd love to,' I replied.

The protest wasn't long after my return from Brighton and back online my followers showed me exactly the same warmth. *Welcome back!* a couple posted that week, mindful that I'd taken a short break and been mainly offline while I'd got my head together by the coast. *So cool to see you again,* another posted. In my mind, I now considered my followers like my online family. It didn't matter that most of us had never met. In many ways it reminded me of the very early days of using chat rooms and being an online gamer when I was back in Washington State – a member of a kind and non-threatening community. What was even more reassuring is that when I'd reached out to them for some understanding they'd allowed me to be human. I didn't have to pretend to be perfect. Now I knew I could have bad days and it would be okay – my followers would accept me, regardless. Gatherings like the LCC protest also reminded me that I now had friends I could check in with all over the city.

As I ran through my film for that day, I remembered back to when Bianca and I had first arrived in London and Sigi had gone missing. As we were roaming the streets searching for her, I recalled how helpless I'd felt. If someone had snatched her, I knew in my heart she'd probably be gone for ever. Now, life had transformed. Whenever we moved through crowds, that same paranoia didn't consume me. I didn't grab hold of Sigi's leash like I had done at the anti-vax protest. If I ever did lose Sigi, I felt convinced that if I put out a call online a search party would descend. Whether it was new friends we'd made in London, Lexi and Mary, the fixed-gear crew, the Fancy Women, the LCC, the Camden punks or friends at The Washington or the Steele, love and luck would come our way.

That November more positive vibes kept landing. Not long before Christmas as Sigi and I were strolling through Camden Town, we were stopped by a film crew dressed in bright yellow hoodies adorned with smiley faces. We'd just come from saying hi to Zombie Punk and we were headed up the main street where Sigi loves being sidetracked in shop doorways.

One guy bent down and pointed a microphone in our direction, pretending to interview Sigi. 'Mind if we do a quick interview?' he joked.

'Sure, where you from?'

'The Smiley Movement,' he said. The guy introduced himself as Harrison and explained that he was the video production guy at the charitable wing of the Smiley Company, which licenses out the universally recognized image of a yellow and black happy face. I had no clue about the company, but apparently it had its own news service that broadcasts good news stories.

'What question do you want to ask?' I looked at him quizzically.

'What's the one thing you'd like to do in the new year?'

Funnily, the answer came easily to me. 'My cat's deaf. I'd like to take her to a deaf school,' I told Harrison.

'Great answer,' he laughed.

The idea had come about because on our regular cycle route through Camden I'd started noticing signs for the Frank Barnes School for Deaf Children. And only a few weeks before Sigi and I had been enjoying a beer with the Fixed Pirates Crew when an elderly lady had approached Sigi. 'Is she deaf?' she'd called over, but at the same time she gestured in what looked like sign language.

'Yeah, she is,' I replied. The woman stayed only for a passing stroke, but she stuck in my mind. As I'd gone through my footage, I concluded that she must have also been deaf and known about the white hair and blue-eyed probability in cats. I don't know why I hadn't thought of it before. Connecting Sigi with members of the deaf community would be amazing.

After the camera clicked off, Harrison asked if we could exchange details. It was his full-time job to arrange hook-ups exactly like the one I'd suggested. If I was happy to leave it with him, he could set the wheels in motion and suggested that if the school were in agreement the news channel would also like to film it. 'Sure, go for it,' I replied. Without even searching for it, Sigi and I had made another connection. 'Always expect the unexpected.' I smiled at Sigi as we carried on walking. It was my new motto for life.

Not long after, Eilidh from the LCC emailed. The campaign was holding its annual awards ceremony in December. It had recently moved to new office space just north of Holborn, and if I wanted to drop by to say hi to the team, Sigi and I could accompany them as special guests to the awards. It was one thing seeing people at protests, but I felt genuinely touched that they had thought to include me.

See you there! I replied.

The meeting was scheduled for the run-up to Christmas and by the time Sigi and I arrived that afternoon it was already dark. The depths of winter in the UK always feel far longer than those in the States. Often the temptation to huddle indoors can be overwhelming but with Sigi and our new life we were constantly forced out, always feeling the benefit for making the effort. To make us feel even more cheerful, however, I'd dressed Sigi in a red Santa suit and decorated her basket in fairy lights.

After we'd pressed the door buzzer a welcoming party arrived downstairs to greet us. Everybody commented on how chilled Sigi was and how unflappable she seemed to be riding around and meeting new people. If only that could have been Sigi's lasting impression. That afternoon, she made her mark for another, less wholesome, reason.

Upstairs in the office Eilidh introduced us and talked me

through some of the LCC's upcoming campaigns. All the while I hadn't been paying attention to Sigi, but when I turned around I found her stretched up on her hind legs, trying to reach a plant positioned behind some desks. 'She loves plants,' I announced. Sigi couldn't quite get hold of the leaves between her teeth, but she did look very determined. I could see her mind working overtime. Finally, she leaped up on to the windowsill, manoeuvring herself into prime position and, in typical Sigi fashion, started chewing.

'Can't take her anywhere,' I said embarrassed. I considered grabbing her, but stupidly decided against it. 'Sig, you can't go around eating other people's plants,' I jokingly told her off.

'It's okay!' Eilidh said kindly, not realizing things were about to get a whole lot worse. Only minutes later Sigi had made her way on to a desk and was heading in the direction of several computers when she stopped still and craned her neck forward. *Oh Jesus*, I thought. *I've seen that look before.* Her body started to heave. Then, there was a wretch . . . then another. *Please don't be sick. Here of all places.* But it was too late. Everyone looked on in horror as Sigi vomited the vandalized plant across the shiny white desk.

'That's one way to christen your new offices. I'm so sorry,' I said apologetically. In truth, I wasn't too concerned for Sigi knowing once she'd thrown up she would feel 100 per cent better. I was more angry with myself for not pulling her away from the plant. I had known some plants are toxic for cats, although that variety had not been on my radar. I should have kept a closer eye on her. 'You okay Sig?' I called over. I could tell that she was a little shaken, but underneath that exterior I also knew Sigi was made of tough stuff.

Fortunately, everyone was understanding, which immediately settled my anxiety. Mel, the digital communications officer, ran to fetch some paper towels and I cleaned the desk. We were guests, after all, so I wasn't going to let anyone else deal with a pile of cat vomit. It smelled disgusting.

The awards were taking place in a cycling-themed bar a ten-minute journey from the LCC offices. As we took our seat I was still apologizing. I checked in on Sigi again. If she was distressed, I'd take her home. 'Hey Sig, feeling better?' I gave her neck a gentle nuzzle. Sigi was still a little subdued but looked happy enough curled up on a chair. As the ceremony began I felt sure the vibration of the compère's voice through the microphone would soothe her. As each winner was read out – individuals who had worked hard within the LCC to lobby authorities and campaign for cyclists across the year – I could see her nodding off.

'Travis, we don't have an award for you and Sigi, but we do appreciate how much you do for us.' Eilidh leaned over as the evening drew to a close.

'Oh no problem! Just happy to help,' I replied. An award was the last thing Sigi and I would have expected but it was lovely to be recognized for being part of a campaign that we felt passionately about.

Over the next few days, snow arrived. It was the first time it had appeared since the months after we landed in London two years previous. The forecast had predicted it, but I was unsure whether it would settle. As the flakes began falling, Sigi and I sat by the front window watching it drift down under the orange glow of the street lights on England's Lane. Two years ago seemed like a very long time. I remembered how Sigi had tentatively made her way down our front steps then refused to move, unsure about the new experience. Now, she seemed fearless accompanying me in all winds and weather. I thought about myself too. How that first Christmas I'd been settling into work, finding my feet and excited about the year ahead. How could I have known what the months and years would bring? Weird to think the pandemic wasn't a reality, neither was my redundancy. Most of all, though, I could never in my wildest dreams have imagined rebuilding my life and my confidence ride by ride with Sigi by my side.

Suddenly, a feeling of calm crept over me. *I love spending every day with you*, I thought as I bent over to give Sigi a kiss. *I love how we make other people happy, too.* Who could have predicted that?

'Shall we head out to play in the snow?' I turned to Bianca who was watching TV. Sigi shot me a hopeful look as I tapped the windowpane and pointed outside.

That night the snow had fallen to at least an inch thick. I wrapped Sigi up in a thick quilted harness and necktie to keep her warm. And as soon as I opened the front door, she barely skipped a beat. Before I knew it she was strutting down each step, pressing her nose against the cold, fresh snow that had blanketed the front garden. She looked like she'd just burst through a wardrobe door and discovered Narnia.

'Not so scared now, huh?' I said, genuinely surprised.

'Throw a snowball!' I shouted to Bianca, feeling mischievous.

Bianca bent down and scooped up the powdery snow and tossed a fluffy ball gently at Sigi, but it ricocheted off her harness and showered over her head.

'That's mean!' I laughed jokingly, but I wasn't worried about Sigi at all. She looked unflappable. She shook the snow off gently and continued dancing down the garden path. 'We've come so far, little one,' I said, encouraging her. Inside, I knew I was speaking for the both of us.

By January 2023, Sigi and I had clocked up 2,500 miles on the bike.

The Frank Barnes School for Deaf Children had responded to The Smiley Movement's request for Sigi and I to visit. Apparently the headmaster Dani bit Harrison's hand off at the offer. And, following an introductory meeting online between myself, Harrison and Dani, a format for the visit was agreed. Two classes would meet Sigi. There would be a chance for them to pet her so long as she was happy, then each visit would be rounded off with a question and answer session where the kids could ask whatever they wanted about Sigi and our life together.

When I logged off, I couldn't help thinking that none of it would be happening without the hard work of Harrison. After that chance meeting on Camden High Street, he had taken my idea and run with it. Serendipity and a good dose of determination, I called it.

On the morning of the visit, I woke feeling more alert than I had done in months. Dani's enthusiasm about the kids meeting Sigrid the deaf cat had rubbed off on me. By the time Sigi and I were on the road, I got another sign it was going to be a great day. On a cycle path a few blocks from the school I saw Sigi's head dart to her right. Suddenly, a black cat appeared and bolted across the road. 'Hey where's this fella going?' I called out.

We followed the cat for a while, making a quick detour up a side street before Sigi hissed at it and it disappeared. I've never been a superstitious person, but I couldn't help wondering about the old saying that black cats bring good luck, although I could see Sigi was more preoccupied with marking out some territory.

'No time for these high-jinks. We've got places to be,' I said, before turning the bike around and continuing on our journey.

The Frank Barnes School for Deaf Children was far more state-of-the-art than I had imagined, with glass-fronted doors and a waiting area filled with pictures and sculptures made by the children. No sooner had we sat down to wait for Dani than Sigi wandered off, lured in by a pot plant. 'No way, Sigi, not today.' I tugged twice on her leash and brought her back.

Staff at the LCC had been so generous, but Sigi throwing up on a classroom of seven-year-olds may not draw the same response. It had to be avoided at all costs. Secretly, too, I was hoping the kids there would naturally identify with a deaf cat and maybe this could be the start of an ongoing relationship. Cat vomit was not going to oil those wheels.

'Great to meet you Travis.' Dani held out his hand as he approached. Dani was deaf himself and spoke through an interpreter by his side. I also made a mental note to face him so that he could lip-read. On the way to the classroom he explained how the school was unique. It is one of the only deaf schools in the country with a bilingual philosophy, meaning children who attend learn both British Sign Language and written and spoken English. 'The kids are really excited,' he told me.

In the classroom, Dani settled Sigi in her own seat at the front before another chair was pulled up next to her for me. Harrison and his team had arrived earlier and he was setting up with his film crew in the corner ready to capture the children's faces. We discussed the format briefly before I heard the hubbub of children get louder as they made their way down the corridor. When they turned into the classroom, their reaction was priceless. As soon as a small group of around 15 kids saw Sigi their eyes almost popped from their heads. Others stopped dead with their mouths agape.

'Look, there's the cat!' I heard a couple whispering to their friends.

Once everyone was settled Dani addressed the class. 'What's happening today?' he asked.

'A deaf cat!' the kids shouted in unison.

At that moment I could feel my heart swell with fatherly pride. Sigi was magical like that, and as she sat purring on the chair, I think she knew it.

After a short introduction the kids lined up to pet Sigi, some more gently than others. I understood they were excited but I did end up having to warn a couple not to stroke Sigi too hard. Her hissing in annoyance wouldn't be a good look. That morning

I'd clipped her claws too, just to be on the safe side. I'd have felt so embarrassed if a child got scratched. Mostly, though, I didn't want them to be scared of Sigi on their first meeting. It needed to be a positive experience. As their pats became gentler, I could hear Sigi purr and watched as her eyes closed with contentment. I marvelled at her patience. It was probably the most kids she'd ever met at once, but she dealt with it as calmly as she did everything else in life.

When it came to the turn of a second class of slightly older kids, they were bursting with interesting questions. One wanted to know how small Sigi was when I adopted her in America.

'Oh she was tiny, around three months old,' I recalled, feeling a twinge of nostalgia.

Another was curious about whether Sigrid was a boy or a girl and asked how I was able to tell.

'Umm . . .' I hesitated. Somehow I doubted it was my place to give a bunch of kids a biology lesson. After an awkward pause, I was relieved when a teacher stepped in and signed an explanation to the class.

Many of the students also assumed that because they were meeting a deaf cat that Sigrid would understand sign language too.

'Have you taught her how to sign?' one asked. On the surface, what seemed like a nonsensical question in fact turned out to have a kernel of truth. Cats are super-clever and can make connections between sounds and signals and words. Owners can train them with multicoloured electronic buttons, each with a different instruction when it is pressed. It's not something

I'd ever done with Sigi, I explained, and it does take time and patience, but pets do figure out which colours or words mean different things, such as: 'Can I have some food?' or 'I want to go for a walk'.

The kids hung off my every word, desperate to know all about Sigi. And, as the session drew to a close, it wasn't hard to see how much love the children had for her.

'Who wants a deaf cat?' Dani asked, as he wrapped up the question and answer session. Suddenly 20 small hands shot up. As far as I was concerned the aim of the day had been achieved. The kids really did identify with Sigi.

'Please do come again,' Dani said.

'Hear that Sigi? We've been invited back,' I joked. Inside I was relieved the visit had gone smoothly. No hissing, no vomit and a roomful of happy kids. Best of all, Harrison was delighted to have captured a great story for the Smiley newsfeed and even suggested that we explore filming a longer series in the future. *Sigi will be in line for an Oscar next*, I thought before I settled her back in her basket.

The visit to the deaf school made a lasting impact on me, and in the coming weeks I thought more about how I could use mine and Sigi's platform again to highlight other issues close to my heart. I'd ticked the cycling box and fulfilled my idea about connecting Sigi with the deaf community. Now it was time to make another awe-inspiring connection.

On Instagram I'd stumbled across a guy called Aidan Phelan, a man who was planning to cycle 3,100 miles from New York to LA. The journey would take him across eight states and three time zones to raise money and awareness of mental health. But Adee wasn't just anyone. He is a hair stylist to the stars, the man who famously created David Beckham's iconic mohawk back in the early 2000s. He also caught my eye because he'd raised more than £2.3 million during the pandemic for NHS workers and distributed almost a hundred thousand boxes of care products to frontline staff as they endured long hours caring for Covid-19 patients. During successive lockdowns, his long-term struggle with depression also led him to start a series of walks called Park Life, aimed at getting people out in the fresh air and exercising. Since starting to speak about my own mental health struggles, I wondered whether he would be willing to meet me to talk about managing the condition and to share his experience. In truth, I hadn't expected a reply, but when I reached out to him a message came almost instantly.

Adee lives in Central London and we agreed to meet in St James's Park and cycle together for a couple of hours. Underneath I was terrified. I'd yet to interview a real celebrity for my feed. When I looked again at Adee's feed, there were pictures of him with Oasis's Liam Gallagher, the actor Paddy Considine and framed pictures of all his celebrity clients. What the hell would he make of me? I worried. Superstar Sigi would have to step in, I thought. At least she could distract him if I got tongue-tied.

When the day came I immediately recognized Adee. Tall with a bushy white beard and bald head, he was wheeling his bike towards us. I took a deep breath, but I needn't have stressed out. The minute he saw Sigi his face said it all – it was love at first sight.

'Great to meet you. Aren't you beautiful?' He bent down and

gave Sigi's head a pat. As a hairdresser to the stars I wondered whether he might be eyeing up Sigi's own mane, tempted to fashion her very own mohawk. The vision made me smile.

'Mind if I record this?' I said, thinking it would be polite to check.

'Yeah, cool,' he replied, before we set off riding and chatting.

As it turned out, Adee and I ended up having one of the most affecting conversations I'd ever had, let alone featured on my feed. He explained how he'd suffered from depression for more than 30 years but how he had managed to keep it hidden for much of that time.

'We become good liars,' I said, knowing exactly what he was describing.

Managing the condition was a constant struggle, he admitted, but it's debilitating effect had lessened for him over the years, especially since he'd discovered the benefits of cycling.

'I've got it down to a stage now where I can get up and get out and it's no longer crucifying me,' he told me.

'That's good to hear,' I replied.

As Adee continued to open up, I also started to feel a deep connection with his story. He had grown up with few opportunities, but had made something of himself. In fact, his star had grown to stratospheric heights. On the surface he was an award-winning guy, but in private he was going through mental anguish.

'Had you thought about ending your life?' I asked, admitting that I had seriously planned to and that it had been a job in London that had saved me.

'Absolutely,' Adee opened up. He went on to tell me that he also had good friends he'd lost through depression, like Keith Flint, the lead singer in the band The Prodigy, who had tragically died battling the illness.

It felt like I was only just starting on my journey to connect with other sufferers – people who understood how life-changing the illness can be. My own experience had also shown me that depression cannot be cured like flu, or a virus. It stays with you, but over time I had also found better ways of managing it. Then, Adee said something that struck a chord.

'People ask me how I've cured myself just because I cycle around and smile and tell people about the positive things in my life, but the demons are still there,' he said.

Immediately, I was transported back to my childhood in the Pacific Northwest and to the years I'd spent in San Francisco chasing an impossible dream, and getting so close to that dream, yet all the time covering up so much of what I was feeling. Then I thought about how my redundancy and the pandemic had almost destabilized me, but how I'd lifted myself out. Whether I recognized it before or not, I'd helped save myself. Mostly, though, I recognized how much I had Sigi to thank for saving me.

Without even trying, she'd given me a reason to keep going. She'd forced me out at a time when I needed it most. She'd given me a structure around my days that could easily have been lost. She'd given me the confidence to meet friends I would never have met. She'd help me rebuild my trust and faith in people. She'd made me a kinder human being. Maybe she'd even allowed me to start accepting myself for the person I truly am.

'It's a proper companionship,' Adee observed as we cycled on through Trafalgar Square.

'One hundred per cent,' I replied, looking down lovingly at Sigi. But Sigi wasn't taking any notice. She had one paw draped over the basket edge. Her head was swaying from side to side and she was calmly watching the world go by. 'We take life day by day.' I smiled. Somehow I knew Sigi was smiling too.

AFTERWORD

By spring 2023, Sigi and I had travelled almost 3,000 miles. We have more than one million followers across TikTok, Instagram, Facebook, Twitter and YouTube, but more importantly we've been out and about meeting many more people. Sigi cheered up striking ambulance staff and nurses who we visited on picket lines across London. We joined a group of bold and fearless women at their Freedom Ride in the centre of the city. Sigi even visited the engine room at Tower Bridge and paid homage to the statue of Dick Whittington's cat in North London. We visited a cat cafe where Sigi got petted by a person dressed as a giant cat. We've appeared in international magazines and been interviewed for UK TV channels and also Japanese TV to celebrate International Cat Day. I eventually caught Covid-19 and Sigi kept me company throughout. And, on my road to recovery, we celebrated Sigi's sixth birthday with a drink at the Steele. We signed a long-term partnership with The Smiley Movement to make a series of videos called Travis and Sigrid Charity Rides, where we ride out every month with a star guest. Mostly, though, Sigi and I have been sprinkling a little magic dust of happiness wherever we go.

ACKNOWLEDGEMENTS

The last couple of years have been both difficult and uplifting, and there are people I would like to thank who have helped me along the way. Without them I would not have been able to share the joy of Sigrid and write this book. Many thanks to Briony Gowlett at Radar who commissioned *Sigrid Rides* after following Sigrid and me online – your enthusiasm has kept me going throughout. All the team at Radar: Sybella Stephens, Clare Hubbard, Elise Solberg, Emily Noto, Rachael Shone, Matt Grindon and Karen Baker, have also been hugely supportive in seeing this project through.

My thanks also go to Helena Drakakis who worked patiently with me on my story and who taught me how to write a book – sometimes travelling over tough terrain. I am also grateful to everybody mentioned in this book: our neighbours who watch us come and go and make this our home; all the witches, pirates and beer drinkers in the fixed-gear scene; the staff and customers at our second home in the Steele, as well as our makeshift office at Chamomile Café, and our ever-supportive friends at the London Cycling Campaign who work tirelessly to make the streets safe for all of us. Special thanks also go to my wife Bianca for putting up with all this craziness, and my departed best friend Teresa whose lessons about life are with me still. Finally, a big thanks goes out to those who have ridden with us or stopped for a chat and given Sigrid a stroke, and to everyone around the world who has taken a moment to watch us ride and share a smile with us.